Netherland Dw.

Netherland Dwarf Rabbits as pets.

Netherland Dwarf Rabbit book including pros and cons, care, housing, cost, diet and health.

By

Macy Peterson

Table of Contents

Introduction

I want to thank you and congratulate you for buying this book. This book will help you to understand everything you need to know about domesticating a Netherland dwarf rabbit. You will learn all the aspects related to raising the Netherland dwarf rabbit successfully at home. You will be able to understand the pros and cons, behavior, basic care, keeping, housing, diet and health related to the animal.

There are people who are impressed by the adorable looks of the Netherland dwarf rabbit. They think that this reason is enough to domesticate the animal, but the domestication of a Netherland rabbit has its unique challenges and issues. If you are not ready for these challenges, then you are not ready to domesticate the animal. If you have already bought or adopted a Netherland dwarf rabbit, even then you need to understand your pet so that you take care of him or her in a better way. It is important that you understand that owning any pet will have its advantages and disadvantages.

You should see whether with all its pros and cons, the animal fits well into your household. Domesticating and taming a pet is not only fun, there is a lot of hard work that goes into it. It is important that you are ready to commit before you decide to domesticate the animal. If you are a prospective buyer, understanding these points will help you to make a wise decision. When you decide to hand raise a Netherland dwarf rabbit, you will be flooded with questions in your head. Would I be able to care for him? Would I be able to domesticate a wild animal? What if I fail in my endeavor? You will find yourself thinking about these and many such questions.

Not matter how scared you are, you can always make it work if you equip yourself with the right knowledge. If you understand how a Netherland dwarf rabbit should be cared for, you will make it work for yourself. You should make all possible efforts to understand the basic requirements of your pet. There are a few basic requirements that you will have to fulfill. Even if you can't afford to give the pet too much luxury, you should be able to take care of his basic requirements.

If you wish to raise a Netherland dwarf rabbit as a pet, there are many things that you need to keep in mind. It can get very daunting for a new owner. Because of the lack of information, you will find yourself getting confused as to what should be done and what should be avoided. You might be confused and scared, but there is no need to feel so confused.

Once you form a relationship with the Netherland dwarf rabbit, it gets better and easier for you as the owner. The pet will grow up to be friendly and adorable. He/she will also value the bond as much as you do. This will be good for the pet and also for you as the pet owner in the long run.

Chapter 1: Understanding a Netherland dwarf rabbit

A Netherland dwarf rabbit is one of the most popular breeds of the domestic rabbits, Oryctolagus cuniculus. These rabbits are known to have originated from the Netherlands, hence the name of the breed.

Netherland dwarf rabbits are known to be very curious, energetic, playful and adorable. They can be clever and timid at the same time. They are ideal for people who are looking for tiny, cute and lovable pets.

It is important that you learn about Netherland dwarf rabbits before you make a decision to domesticate them because they are not for everybody. You don't want to get an animal home and later regret your decision.

This chapter and the subsequent chapters will help you to understand the history and some interesting facts about these cute and adorable animals. You will also get some practical knowledge about hand raising these animals.

The Netherland dwarf rabbit can get nervous very easily. They can get uneasy and can slip into depression if not looked after.

These rabbits enjoy the company of human beings and are known to have a good time with them, but they should be trained to socialize from an early age. If they don't socialize from the beginning, they can develop aggression towards human beings and other animals.

These rabbits are very popular in shows. Many crosses and Netherland dwarf derived breeds are also very popular amongst pet enthusiasts and rabbit show participants.

1. A brief history of Netherland dwarf rabbits

As the owner or prospective owner of a Netherland dwarf rabbit, you be interested to know that Netherland dwarf rabbits all around the world actually originate from Netherlands. They were first produced in the beginning of 20th century.

Polish rabbits and small wild rabbits were bred for several generations. The result was a very small, domestic rabbit in various colors and patterns. This was the Netherland dwarf rabbit.

It is also known that Netherland dwarf rabbits came to the United States of America in the 1960s. They came to the United Kingdom much earlier, around 1948.

In 1969, ARBA took the decision to categorize Netherland dwarf rabbits as a modification of British rabbits. Captive breeding became very popular in the United States. This meant that a lot of Netherland dwarf rabbits were available.

2. Body structure

Netherland dwarf rabbits are very small in size. They are in fact amongst the smallest of rabbits. The Netherland dwarf rabbit has a compact body and curved profile and its legs are short and rounded.

The head is round in shape. The head and eyes are bigger in comparison to the body. The ears have a peculiar shape and are erect. The structure of the ears helps the rabbit to protect itself from many bacteria and infections.

The coat of the Netherland dwarf rabbit is short and soft. The rabbit comes in different coat colors such as black, white, blue, chocolate, lilac, fox, tortoiseshell, sable marten, Siamese sable, chestnut, agouti, Siamese smoke pearl, fawn, sable point, Himalayan, steel, lynx, broken pattern opal, tan, squirrel, chinchilla, otter, orange, silver marten and smoke pearl marten.

The weight of an average built adult Netherland dwarf rabbits is only around 900 grams.

The small size of the rabbit makes it ideal as a pet and also as an exhibition animal. However, this small size also constricts its use as a primary source of fur and meat.

3. Life span of Netherland dwarf rabbits

A healthy Netherland dwarf rabbit can live from 7 to over 12 years. It is known that a rabbit that is cared for and groomed in a good way and that is kept indoors will have a good life span.

The key is to provide them the right environment and also the right nutrition. This will help them to grow, stay healthy and live longer.

4. General body types of the rabbits

It is known that different types of rabbits have different body types and sizes. An idea of these body types will help you to understand the structure of the Netherland dwarf rabbits in a better way.

Full arch body type

One of the body types of the rabbits is the full arch body type. The full arch body type is very agile and active. They are inclined to be very energetic.

The arch of the rabbit begins at the nape of the neck and continues over the shoulders and the hips in an unbroken and fluid line. This line rounds as it reaches the base of the tail. The ears of the rabbit are erect and the fur is spotted.

The side profile can be visibly seen tapering from the hindquarters to the shoulders. Some of the popular breeds of rabbits possessing this body type are the Rhinelander and English spot.

Compact Body type

Compact body type rabbits are smaller in length and are also lighter in weight compared to the other rabbits. You can also notice a rise in the top line of these bunnies because the depth of the shoulders is less than the depth of the hips.

They appear to be well balanced in their looks. Some compact body type rabbits are the mini satin, mini lop, the Havana and the Dutch.

Semi arch or Mandolin body type

Some rabbits possess the semi arch body type. This body type is also called the gentle giant. This body type represents the large bodies of the bunnies.

The shoulders of this body type are lower and the hip is at a higher level. The side profile can be seen to be tapering from the hindquarters to the shoulders. Some of the popular breeds of rabbits possessing this body type are the Flemish giant and the American.

Commercial Body type

This body type is used for production and meat. The rabbits with these body types grow very fast in comparison to other body types.

Commercial body type rabbits are equally deep and wide in their appearance. They look similar to the compact body type.

Some commercial body type rabbits are the Rex, the Satin, the Silver fox, the French lop and the Giant Angora rabbit.

Cylindrical Body type

There is only one rabbit breed that is categorized under the cylindrical body type, which is the Himalayan rabbit. The Himalayan rabbit is small in size. The body of this breed of rabbit is cylindrical and quite similar to Californian rabbit.

5. Colors and patterns of Netherland dwarf rabbits

It is known that Netherland dwarf rabbits come with various colors and also various patterns.

Self-colored pattern

The self-colored type refers to the rabbit that has a single color all over the body. The various colors in this pattern are white, blue, brown, lilac, red and black.

Shaded pattern

In this type, there is a main color. There is a gradual change from this main color, as the shade keeps getting lighter. The sides and belly typically have the lighter shade of color. The various colors in this pattern include sable medium, sable light, smoke pearl and chocolate point.

Agouti pattern

This pattern has typically three or even more colors. There is a dark base color and alternating colors run through the base color. The various colors in this pattern include chestnut, opal, squirrel, cinnamon, red agouti, lynx and chinchilla.

6. Types of Netherland dwarf rabbits based on coat type

If you are looking to buy a Netherland dwarf rabbit, then you should know that these rabbits have two different kinds of coats or manes. An understanding of this will help you to know the type and kind of your rabbit.

Single Mane rabbits

These kinds of rabbits have a single gene that can produce the coat. This coat keeps depleting as the rabbit ages. You can expect the coat to wear out and thin hairs to remain after a few years.

A thick crimping can be found near the ears, chin and head of the rabbit. You can also spot it in the rump and chest.

Double Mane rabbits

Double mane rabbits are known to have two copies of the mane gene. The wool is thicker compared to single mane rabbits. Thick wool can be expected near the head and flank.

When two single mane rabbits are bred, a double mane rabbit is born. When two double mane rabbits are bred, even then a double man rabbit is born.

7. Pros and cons of keeping Netherland dwarf rabbits

If you wish to hand raise an animal, you should make sure that you understand the characteristics and the requirements of the animal. When you domesticate the Netherland dwarf rabbit, you will face many pros and cons along the way.

This section will help you understand the pros and cons of keeping a Netherland dwarf rabbit at home.

Pros of keeping a Netherland dwarf rabbit at home

There are many pros of keeping a Netherland dwarf rabbit:

- These rabbits enjoy the company of human beings and are known to have a good time with them.

- These pets are great for smaller living spaces, such as a flat or small house.

- These pets are generally low maintenance. They do not need frequent baths, which can be a great relief for a caregiver.

- A rabbit is a very intelligent and smart animal. You can easily train him/her to suit your family and living conditions.

- The rabbit is beautiful to look at. If you are fond of beautiful looking pets, then this rabbit is definitely the pet for you and your family.

- The rabbits are very energetic and lively pets. They are very active during the early hours of the morning and evening.

- The rabbits are very sweet, entertaining and gentle in their nature, yet they need to be trained well so that they don't get too mischievous. You will also get to see the calm, composed and gentle side of the animal.

- If they are raised to be social, they will be very social. You should make sure that they spend a lot of time indoors with the family members. This will only help in being more social and affectionate.

- The rabbit is a very playful, happy-go-lucky kind of animal. The rabbit likes having fun and can be a constant source of entertainment for everyone in the family.

- You can enter your pet in various shows that happen everywhere. These are shows that can help you gain popularity and can help you win also.

- They are capable of forming strong emotional bonds. These bonds will last for a lifetime. You need to spend quality time with your pet to form such strong bonds.

- You will find it easier to groom the pet because he/she will be relaxed and calm, unlike many other pets that don't allow the owners to groom them.

- It has been established over the years that the rabbits are easy to train.

- When you domesticate a rabbit, you will have to worry less about diet. This is because nowadays many diet mixtures and pellets are available commercially. These food items ensure that the right nutrition is given to your beloved pet. You can be happy because you can save yourself from the tension of preparing food mixes for the pet every now and then.

- You would have to be extra careful and cautious while taking care of the kit, but when all the precautions are taken, it is a very much possible task to hand raise a bunny or kit.

- They will respond to the way you choose to communicate with them. If you provide good training to your rabbit, you will notice that he/she responds well. In due time and over the course of the training, the pet will also start obeying some simple commands that you would want them to obey.

Cons of keeping a Netherland dwarf rabbit at home

There are many cons of keeping a Netherland dwarf rabbit:

- The Netherland dwarf rabbit can get nervous and frightened very easily. They can get uneasy and can slip into depression if not looked after.

- These rabbits enjoy the company of human beings and are known to have a good time with them. But, they should be trained to socialize from an early age. If they don't socialize from the beginning, they can develop aggression towards human beings and other animals.

- Bigger animals can make the Netherland dwarf rabbit prey.

- You can't keep these animals in a cage at all times. They need space and time to explore and play.

- If the rabbit is not under supervision, it can get very mischievous. The animal will chew at things, even electrical wiring.

- The pet is also prone to many diseases. The caregiver will have to be very careful with the health of the pet.

- The pet can get stressed and depressed if it is left lonely for long durations. You can't leave it in the cage for too long.

- The bunnies love to dig in the ground. In fact, the rabbit will try to dig every place. If the pet is left on its own, it might try to dig in your sofas, beds, etc.

- If you don't have the time and energy to spend on grooming a pet, then the Netherland dwarf rabbit is not the right pet for you.

- If the children of the house are not careful, they can scare the pet. This can be detrimental to the Netherland dwarf rabbit.

- The cost that you will incur while buying and raising is more when compared to other pets, such as the dog and the cat. If spending too much money is an issue with you, then you will have to think twice before purchasing the animal.

- These animals love playing and running around. These pets are fond of exploring things and can create a mess if not monitored.

Chapter 2: Things to know before you buy a Netherland dwarf rabbit

Before you buy a Netherland dwarf rabbit and bring him home to hand raise him, it is important that you understand certain facts regarding these animals. (Please note that although you can have females, we shall refer to them as 'he' for ease). You should understand their behavior and also the cost incurred in domesticating them. Having knowledge of all these things will help you to make a better decision regarding the domestication of the Netherland dwarf rabbit.

1. Costs

You should also be prepared on the financial front to take care of these needs. It is better that you plan these things well in advance. This planning will help you to avoid any kind of disappointment that you might face when there are some payments that need to be made.

There are basically two kinds of costs that you will be looking to incur, which are as follows:

- **The one-time or initial costs**: The initial costs are the ones that you will have to bear in the very beginning of the process of domestication of the animal. This will include the one-time payment that you will give to buy the animal.
- **The regular or monthly costs**: The monthly costs are the ones that you will have to spend each month or once in few months. This category includes the costs of the food requirements and health requirements of the pet. The various regular veterinarian visits, the sudden veterinarian visits and replacement of things come under the monthly category.

Purchase price: You can expect to spend $20/£15.16 to $250/£184.97 to purchase your rabbit. The price will depend on the color, age and the health of the Netherland dwarf rabbit. It is also possible to get one for as low as $15/£11.37 from a backyard breeder, but then you can never be sure of the quality of the pet breed.

In general, a good quality Netherland dwarf rabbit can be bought for $50/£37.91. If the bunny is neutered or spayed, expect to pay even around $150/£113.72. If you wish to get a quality fit for shows, you can expect a price even above $200/£151.63.

You should make sure that you get the bunny examined medically before buying it. The examination and tests will also add on to the initial price.

You also have the option to adopt a bunny. This will help you to avoid the initial purchasing price, though the other costs for raising the animal will remain essentially the same.

If your breeder has taken care of the initial health check-ups, then you should be fine with paying a little extra to this breeder because he/she has saved you from running here and there to get these important procedures done.

Rabbit hutch or cage: When you look for a cage or hutch for the Netherland dwarf rabbit, you will realize that there are great options available for cages in pet shops. You can buy a cage for as low as $35/£26.54 and also as high as $500/£378.25. It clearly depends on your choice and your budget. A decent cage can be expected at $160/£121.30.

The cage is a basic requirement for a pet animal even if you plan to keep him indoors most of the time. A pet should be provided with a comfortable cage. It is always better to get a bigger cage for the comfort of the pet. The floor of the cage should be solid. The size and material have a direct effect on the cost of the cage.

Toys: As an important accessory for the pet's cage, you will have to invest in good quality toys. Cheap plastic materials that can have an adverse effect on the health of the bunny must be avoided. Similarly, toys that can be shredded or broken should also be avoided.

Depending on your choice of toys, you can expect to spend about $50/£36.99 to $250/£184.97.

Water and food containers: You will have to buy food and water containers for your pet animal. They will be included in the initial costs. It is important that you should invest in good quality containers so that you don't have to buy replacement containers in a few months.

The containers should be bought to suit the animal's requirements. You should plan the number of containers that you would need. The estimated cost for the food and water container can be $100/£73.99 to $250/£184.97.

Bedding: The bedding for the pet is another important purchase. If you buy liners, you can expect to spend $30/£22.20 to $60/£44.39 once. If you go for paper bedding, you will have to spend $50/£36.99 to $100/£73.99 per year.

Litter box: You will have to buy one or more litter boxes for the rabbit. You also have to use paper litter shavings to train the pet well for using the litter box. Depending on whether you make the litter box at home or purchase it from the pet store, you can expect to spend $1/£0.74 to $10/£7.40.

Food: A domesticated rabbit will mostly be fed hay, grass and vegetables. You might also have to include various pellets and supplements to give your pet overall nourishment.

You should feed about two cups of greens per day to the rabbit. This should cost you around $10/£7.68 per month. You can expect to pay $3/£2.32 to $5/£3.84 for the pellets.

You should make sure that there is enough fiber in the diet of the Netherland dwarf rabbit. You need to feed timothy hay to the Netherland dwarf rabbit every day. This should cost you about $3/£2.32 per month.

Vet fund: A yearly check-up will help you keep track of the health and progress of your pet. This yearly visit, that also includes tests, should not cost you more than $60/£44.39. This is a cost that you have to pay once a year, but it is better to plan it well ahead of time.

You should also be prepared for unexpected costs, such as sudden illness or accidents. Healthcare is provided at different prices in different areas, so the veterinarian in your area could be costlier than the veterinarian in the nearby town.

Though it is always advised to take the pet to the vet if any health problem arises, it is always a great idea to keep a first aid kit ready. You can expect to spend around $50/£36.99 to $60/£44.39 while preparing a basic first aid box for the bunny.

It is believed that you should have an extra $1000/£776.2 saved for your pet's emergencies. He might require an operation or surgery because of a disease, for example.

2. Netherland dwarf rabbit Insurance

You can get insurance for your Netherland dwarf rabbit. This insurance will help you to take care of the veterinarian bills and injury costs. A sudden procedure can cost you over thousands of pounds or dollars, so it better to insure the rabbit.

Depending on the insurance you buy, you can also cover regular clinic visits. There are some companies that will give you discounts on clinic visits. There are some companies that can help you with rabbit insurance, such as Exotic direct, pet plan and NCI. These companies have different kinds of insurance.

Rabbit insurance can cost you around $8/£6.14 to $20/£15.35 per month. The exact amount will depend on the company that you choose and also on the area where you live. For example, in southeast London you will be required to pay $20/£15.35.

You can choose according to your requirements. You can also get a package deal if you are looking to insure more than one rabbit. When you buy insurance, you have to pay a deductible amount and regular premiums. You will also be required to pay premiums that need to be paid regularly to keep the insurance policy active.

3. Neutering or spaying

Neutering or spaying has become an important part of pet domestication. As an owner, you need to make a decision whether you would want your pets to have progenies or not.

Netherland dwarf rabbits can be neutered or spayed by the owners or the breeders. When you are sure that you don't want your doe to breed, it is better to spay the animal before it is too late. Similarly, neuter the male if you don't want breeding.

It should also be understood that neutering or spaying the rabbit will have its consequences on the pet. It is better to understand these consequences. Talk to the veterinarian about them and be prepared for them.

It is known that males get less aggressive if they are neutered at the right age. It is advised to get the process done before it is four months old. If the rabbit is an adult, neutering or spaying will have a lot of complications, which you would definitely want to avoid.

The sexual organs of the rabbits are located towards the inside and the animal is also very small. The entire process can be very tricky and complicated. It is extremely important that you get the neutering or spaying done by a trained professional who has experience dealing with these animals.

4. Understanding the rabbit's behavior

It is important to understand the behavior and temperament of the specific animal that you wish to domesticate. This will help you to be a better master. Your Netherland dwarf rabbit might still have some surprises for you, but it is better to know of the general behavior of the animal.

A Netherland dwarf rabbit is a small and naughty animal that will keep you busy and entertained by all its unique antics and mischiefs. It is said that each animal is different from the other. Each one will have some traits that are unique to him.

While you will learn about all the unique traits that your particular bunny has by experiencing him and spending time with him, there are some traits that almost all Netherland dwarf rabbits will exhibit.

It is beneficial to know of these traits so that you are not taken off guard. You will be able to understand what is normal for this animal and what is not. This will help you to be more prepared and not be confused every time something happens.

The following personality traits will help you to be better prepared for your pet Netherland dwarf rabbit:

Licking each other

If you are planning to domesticate more than one Netherland dwarf rabbit, then this is one antic that you will notice a lot in your Netherland dwarf rabbits. Rabbits love to lick each other. Actually, this is a good sign. This means that the pets like each other and are getting along.

You might find them making sounds of excitement. Don't worry because this is very normal behavior in rabbits. However, do keep an eye on the pets so that things don't go out of hand.

Thumping

When a Netherland dwarf rabbit thumps his hind legs furiously, it means that he is scared. A Netherland dwarf rabbit that has taken up a corner and is thumping while making noises is definitely scared.

This could happen if the pet is somewhere for the very first time. This could also happen if the pet is involved in a very high intensity play. You can expect your pet to be all charged up like a rocket at this time. You will notice immense amounts of energy in him. He will dart from one end to another in seconds and you should just forget about catching up with him.

Binkying

One of the most popular and endearing traits of the Netherland dwarf rabbits is its dance of excitement. This is called binkying. When a bunny is all excited, he will jump and flip. He will dart from one side to another. You might see him jumping from the top of furniture. This is the dance of excitement of the rabbit.

The rabbit might also emit certain kinds of sounds during this dance. This is a simple indication for you that the pet is very excited and happy and wants to play and have some fun with you.

A new owner might not take well to this unique way of displaying excitement. There are many owners and their family members who get scared after seeing the bunny like this. You should know that this behavior is completely normal and the Netherland dwarf rabbit will not harm you. He is just having fun and wants to include you in his fun.

Digging

There are certain traits that are ingrained in an animal. No matter how unwanted and troublesome that might seem to you, but you have to get used to it. One such trait in the bunny is digging. Bunnies are very fond of digging.

While it is okay if they try to dig a blanket or the ground in the open yard, it can be troublesome if they try to dig their food. When you serve food to them in a food bowl, they will get all excited and will try to dig the food. This will not result in anything but a lot of mess.

They might try to dig on your leg or shoulder. This is a way to gain your attention. As an owner, you can just ignore this habit of the pet because it comes naturally to him. Many people might get disturbed by this habit of the pet, but it is better to just get used to it as soon as possible.

Nipping

Netherland dwarf rabbits have a tendency to nip. You should know that this is absolutely normal for a rabbit and that you can slowly train the rabbit not to exhibit such behavior. It is important that you understand the reason behind a pet's nipping. You should not harm the pet when he nips. This could scare him and will make things worse for you.

More often than not, pets do so when they are in a playful mood. If your rabbit wants you to play with him, he could just signal you to do so by nipping. Such behavior is quite common in younger rabbits.

Another reason behind a pet's nipping is that the animal could be scared. When you bring the pet to your home for the first time, everything around him will be new. It is quite natural for the pet to get scared. This is the reason that nipping is very common in a new pet.

Sniffing or nose bonking/nudging

You might observe a rabbit sniffing around stuff. This is his way of getting used to things around him. This will look particularly entertaining to many people, as the pet tries very hard, but in the end gets nowhere. Don't worry, as this is just one of the plays of the Netherland dwarf rabbit.

This technique is also a way of establishing supremacy for a rabbit. A strong and dominant Netherland dwarf rabbit will nudge the other rabbits to let them know that he is the boss in the household.

Chinning

A rabbit might rub his chin over you or other things. This is called chinning. The chin of the rabbit has scent glands. When he rubs his chin, the glands get activated, releasing scents. This is his way of marking his territory.

This technique is basically a way of establishing supremacy for a rabbit. A strong and dominant Netherland dwarf rabbit will mark his territory to let the other rabbits know that he is the boss in the household.

The dominant rabbit will try his antics on the poor submissive one. You will find them making sounds of excitement. Don't worry because this is very normal behavior in rabbits. Yet, do keep an eye on the animals so that things don't go out of hand.

Screaming or growling

When the Netherland dwarf rabbit is frightened or angry, it will make noises that sound like a hiss. This is known as screaming. Again, you have to closely observe your pet to understand his moods and the accompanying sounds.

When you see a sad or angry pet, your first instinct as the parent would be to pick the pet up and calm him down. But, you are advised not to do so. When a pet is angry, he needs some time to calm down. If you get over protective, he might just get irritated and bite you out of frustration.

You should say some kind and soothing words to the pet. Your tone will make him realize that you care for him. After that just leave the area. The pet needs some time. He will utilize this time and will cool down on his own.

Another point to be noted here is that an over excited pet might also make a similar noise. When two or more rabbits are left to play with each other, they could emit a sound quite similar to hissing. It is important that you understand whether the pet is angry, scared or just having fun.

You can use a simple trick to know whether the pet is angry or not. You should pay attention to the rabbit's body language. If the rabbit is sticking to a corner, is making noises, has a bent or arched back and has his fur standing, then the animal is definitely upset and needs time to calm down.

Grinding teeth

Another trait that you can expect from your pet rabbit is the grinding of the teeth. This is a very lovable feature. They grind their teeth in excitement or happiness.

You can notice this behavior in rabbits when they get along well with each other and when they are playing with each other. For example, the rabbit will grind his teeth when it is having a good play with another rabbit the house.

Sometimes, the pet can grind his teeth ferociously to express anger. You should pay attention to the rabbit's body language.

5. Breeding in Netherland dwarf rabbits

Mating can be a complicated process in Netherland dwarf rabbits, so you need to be prepared for it. A lot of patience will be required from the owner during the entire procedure.

It is known that the Netherland dwarf rabbit is a very limited breed. Their breeding can lead to the untimely death of the female rabbit or stillborn kits. Some kits will die after the process of weaning.

Basic breeding information for Netherland dwarf rabbits

Each animal species has their unique breeding habits and patterns. When you are looking to take care of your pet well, you should also lay enough emphasis on understanding its breeding patterns.

A good breeder will always encourage you to thoroughly understand the sexual tendencies of your rabbits, so as to not commit any mistakes in the future. You need to know how often and in what conditions your rabbits can reproduce.

You should make sure that the rabbits are not overweight when they are ready for mating. An overweight rabbit will only add to the complexity of breeding. An obese female rabbit can't release eggs properly because of the fat around her ovaries.

The overweight rabbit might turn off the other rabbit sexually. So, make sure they are healthy and attractive. In addition, the female rabbit shouldn't be too small. This will pose a danger to her health when she gives birth to the kits.

Spring is considered as the best time for breeding in the Netherland dwarf rabbit. If you are mating the Netherland dwarf rabbits in summer, make sure that you have climate control in the cage.

Excessive heat can cause the ears of the newborn rabbits to expand. Similarly, invest in climate control and light cycle control if you are looking to mate the Netherland dwarf rabbits in winter.

Even after the mating is done, it is important that the rabbits are exposed only to controlled environments. If the rabbit is forced to be in an environment that is too hot, it will not be able to mate for at least a month.

It is important to note that the reproductive system of Netherland dwarf rabbits is very different from most other animals. The rabbits are induced ovulators. The eggs are not released until the process of mating takes place. The eggs will be released after approximately ten hours of mating.

The male and female Netherland dwarf rabbits get sexually mature by six to seven months of age. It is important that they are bred within the first year of their birth because after that their pelvic bones will automatically fuse.

Breeding can help the rabbits to remain healthy. Breeding helps the female rabbit to ward off the danger of uterine cancer in later years of her life. If the female is not bred in the first year, it is difficult for her to give birth to a healthy litter.

Mating behavior of the Netherland dwarf rabbits

You should understand the natural mating behavior of your Netherland dwarf rabbits. This will help you to do the right thing while breeding them.

A female Netherland dwarf rabbit is able to produce many kits at a single time. It should be understood that rabbits are able to follow one mating cycle with the other in short durations of times.

The rabbits enter their mating cycle in warmer temperatures. You can expect the same when the rabbits are domesticated.

When a rabbit is in its natural environment, the extra amount of light during the summers and also spring brings about a change in its body. The male and female rabbits get sexually active during this time.

A male rabbit will display changes in its behavior. It will seem more aggressive and restless. This is due to the sex hormones that have become active in its body. This is how you can identify if your male rabbit is ready to mate or not.

Another interesting behavior that can be noted in the males is that they become more competitive with other male rabbits. The males that are sexually active compete with each other to establish dominance in the group. This is done so that they can impress the female and attract her for mating.

It is known that in the wild, the dominant male will have a good sex life in comparison to the shy ones. When you see your pet male getting too aggressive and competitive, you should know that he is ready for mating.

When your male rabbit and female rabbit are ready for mating, you should bring the female rabbit to the male rabbit's cage. It should be noted that the opposite should not be done. You should not take the male rabbit to the female rabbit's cage because the female rabbit can get territorial. You might find the female attacking and harming the male instead of mating with him.

Once the male rabbit (buck) is able to attract the female rabbit (doe), the mating can begin. During the process, the female will lie down on a level surface on the ground as an invitation to the male rabbit. The female will also lift its tail.

The male will mount the female rabbit at this time. The mating process can look very funny and clumsy to a first timer. It is advised to keep an eye on them from a distance even if you don't like the act.

You should separate the two once the process is over. Once the female is pregnant, the gestation period in the female will last for over a month. Once that is over, you can expect your pregnant doe to give birth to kits or bunnies.

It should be noted that the newborn kits are hairless. They are also blind at this time. The female is capable of repeating the same process and giving birth to bunnies many times a year.

Kindling and nesting

When you are conducting controlled mating in your home, there are many things that you will have to take care of. You should make sure that the male and the female rabbit are in the same cage when they both are ready.

After they have mated, you should be ready to take care of the doe. It is also important that you take care of the nesting requirements of the rabbits once the mating is over and the female rabbit is pregnant.

The nesting box is a box that will be used by the female rabbit as the nest. She will give birth to the bunnies in the nest. You should make sure that the box is big enough to allow the rabbit to be comfortable. The young ones will spend a lot of time in the nesting box, so it should be as comfortable as possible.

You should only place the nesting box in the rabbit cage when the time is right. If you introduce it any earlier, the rabbit will try to dig it as if it were digging a burrow. The rabbit might also use the box as a litter box. Make sure that this does not happen.

The kindling is expected after one month of the female getting pregnant. Therefore, you should ideally keep the nesting box in the cage on the twenty-eighth day after mating has taken place.

The female is expected to give birth anytime from the twenty-eighth to the thirty-first day after mating. Of course, the mating should have been successful.

You should put some soft pine and hay in the nest box before keeping it in the cage of the rabbit. This will give a cushion like structure to the nest and will make the nest box cozy and comfortable.

There is a natural tendency of the female rabbit that is about give birth: she will pull out some hair from under her chin. This will be used as a cushion for the young ones that are to arrive.

After the female rabbit gives birth to the buns in the nest, she will try to spend most of the time outside the nest. You will see her in the cage, but outside the nest box. The mother will get into the box to feed the babies. You can expect this to happen at least twice a day.

After three weeks, you will see that the babies have started coming out of the nest. They will keep hopping in and out of the nest box at this time.

When you notice that the bunnies are spending a good amount of time outside the box, you should remove the box. The kits don't need it anymore.

6. Purchasing a Netherland dwarf rabbit

Once you have made up your mind whether you want to buy the Netherland dwarf rabbit or not, the next obvious step is to look for the right place to buy it. You can do so from a pet store or directly from a breeder.

Before you buy your Netherland dwarf rabbit, it is important that you do your research well. You should also have the right information about various pet stores and breeders in your state.

You can visit various pet stores to look for the kind of Netherland dwarf rabbit that you are looking for. The local veterinarian can give his/her recommendations in this case. It is always advisable to buy a Netherland dwarf rabbit from a reputable breeder.

The problem with pet stores is that you would not come to know about the history of the rabbit, which is so important to understand the health of the animal. You will also not be able to understand the breeding process and conditions of the animal. These are some important factors in determining the health and the history of the animal.

Buying a rabbit from a breeder has its many benefits. You can talk to the breeder about the many concerns that you might have. You can understand the breeding procedure of the animal and can also be sure that the animal has been in safe hands before you.

You should also make sure that you select the right breeder to buy the rabbit from. It is as important as buying the right pet. If you choose a wrong breeder, you will only have to face problems in the future.

It will pay to talk to other people who have bought rabbits in your region. They could help you in deciding on the right breeders.

There are some breeders who are in this profession for the love of Netherland dwarf rabbits and animals in general. Of course they wish to earn money, but not by compromising their prime duty as a breeder.

You will also find breeders who do this only for the sake of money. Such breeders will not hesitate in providing you with the wrong information about the rabbit to make a few bucks. You need to save yourself from such selfish breeders.

It is important that you devote some time in looking for breeders in and around your region. You should understand the reputation of the breeder before you choose him/her to buy your rabbit.

As the potential buyer, you should know every little detail about your pet animal. You need to make sure that the breeder you choose to buy the Netherland dwarf rabbit from shares all the details about the rabbit.

A good breeder will always ask you questions and will make sure that the animal will get a good owner and a good home. You can expect this from a breeder to cares enough for the animals that he/she keeps.

The breeder would want to understand the prime motive behind your buying the rabbit. He/she would also want to understand if you have the time and energy to devote to the rabbit. The Netherland dwarf rabbit can be demanding as a pet, and you should make sure that you can provide for it.

There have been cases where the breeders have denied permission to the prospective owners because they didn't seem able to provide well for the animal. So if your breeder is asking you questions about how you intend to keep the animal, then this is a good sign.

The breeder will also give you a set of instructions that will come in handy when you are taking care of the rabbit. You should make sure that you understand these instructions well.

List of rescue websites

You also have the option of adopting a rabbit. There are some factors that will govern the final choice that you make. You should make sure that you understand these factors, so that you can make the right choice for yourself as the owner of a new pet.

Many rabbits are mistreated and abandoned by their owners. You can help to give one of these abandoned rabbits a new home. The abandoned rabbit will get a new home and your family will get a new pet.

If you want to buy a kit or younger rabbit, then you should buy him from a good breeder. If you are looking to bring an older rabbit to your home, then you should try to go for adoption.

If you are looking at the financial side of the deal, then you can benefit from adopting the rabbit. Many a times, you can expect to get a cage and other accessories with the abandoned rabbit. This will save you from building or buying a new cage for the animal.

Most adult Netherland dwarf rabbits are vaccinated and litter trained. They are also spayed or neutered. This will also help you to save some money.

If you are looking for reputed breeders, then the following list can help you:

- Rabbit haven: https://therabbithaven.org

- Bunnies are us: www.bunniesareus.com

- Dwarf R US: www. dwarfsrus.com

- Rabbit breeders: http://rabbitbreeders.us

- Evergreen farm: www.evergreenfarm.biz

- Friends of rabbits: www.friendsofrabbits.org

7. Licensing requirements

It is important to understand the licensing rules of Netherland dwarf rabbits. You should be sure that the laws permit you to hand raise the animal. This is important because the law prohibits the domestication of certain animals.

You should understand each detail of the permitting laws before you go and buy the Netherland dwarf rabbit. If you domesticate an animal against the law, the penalty could even include seizure of the animal.

It is important that you understand that the steps of obtaining the license would essentially be the same in most places; there could be slight variations between the various regions.

United States licensing

If you are looking to domesticate a Netherland dwarf rabbit in the United States of America, you need to understand the licensing rules in the country. You don't need a license in most parts of United States to domesticate a Netherland dwarf rabbit.

Private breeders who wish to breed and sell rabbits for profit will have to follow different regulations. You definitely require a license if you are using rabbits for research purposes.

It should be noted that certain areas require you to have a permit or license. Minnesota requires a person to acquire a permit at $15/£11.37 per year if he/she wishes to domesticate a Netherland dwarf rabbit. If the Netherland dwarf rabbit is not spayed or neutered, you can expect to pay even more.

If you wish to register your rabbit, you will have to contact the rabbit clubs on your own. This will allow you to show your rabbit.

It should be noted that all the dealers and breeders that make more than $600/£459.96 will have to get a USDA license. The commercial producers who sell the rabbits to pet stores should be licensed under the rules of AWA.

It is advised that you consult the local municipal hall of your area to know the exact rules and regulations for domestication of the Netherland dwarf rabbits.

United Kingdom licensing

The rules in the United Kingdom are different from those in the United States. The United Kingdom does not require you to obtain a license to keep a Netherland dwarf rabbit.

If you are importing or exporting a Netherland dwarf rabbit, then you need a license. The state would want to verify that the animal that you are planning to import or export is free from diseases such as rabies.

You can also expect an inspector to visit you and your rabbit to make sure that you adhere to all the rules. So, you should make sure that you fulfill all the criteria set by the law.

8. Bringing home a healthy pet

Many a times, people get so excited about buying the animal that they forget to do the basic checks that need to be done before bringing the animal to their house. You should definitely do all the checks before you buy the Netherland dwarf rabbit to avoid any future hassle.

There are many challenges that you will face while raising an animal at home. Your pet might face health issues that you would have to take care of. But, the last thing you want to do is to bring an unhealthy animal home.

It is always advised to discuss the health and also the history of the animal with the breeder before you buy the animal. A good breeder will not hesitate in sharing with you all the details about the animal.

You should make sure that you understand the various health issues that your future pet has suffered. If you are buying a Netherland dwarf rabbit that is older in age then it is all the more important to make sure that you understand the history of the animal. Discuss in length the various issues of the animal.

There are a few checks that you can conduct before you buy the Netherland dwarf rabbit. The following checks will help you to make sure that your rabbit is in good health and condition:

- To begin with, check the coat of the animal. You should look for any abrasions on the Netherland dwarf rabbit's skin. His skin should not be bruised anywhere.

- You should closely look for any injuries on the Netherland dwarf rabbit. If you find a mark or injury, make sure that you understand the cause of it. If it is a temporary issue, then it is fine. Discuss it with the breeder to make sure that the mark is not the indication of a serious issue with the Netherland dwarf rabbit's health.

- The fur of the Netherland dwarf rabbit is the indication of its health. If the fur is soft and shiny, you can be sure that the animal is healthy. One the other hand, if the fur is not good, then the pet has health issues for sure.

- Another simple check that you can perform on your rabbit is to check the body temperature of the Netherland dwarf rabbit. The body temperature should neither be too high or too low. Make sure you discuss the right temperature range of the rabbit with your breeder.

- You should look for any hanging limbs in the animal. This is a clear indication of something being wrong with the animal. A hanging part of the body could mean that the pet is severely injured.

- You should also check the animal's eyes. The eyes should not be dull, they should be bright and shiny. This can also be an indication to the animal's current health.

9. Netherland dwarf rabbits and other pets

If you are keen on domesticating Netherland dwarf rabbits with other pet animals, then it is important that you understand the temperament of the various animals.

Number of Netherland dwarf rabbits you can keep

If you are planning on keeping more than one Netherland dwarf rabbit, you should understand their behavioral and spatial requirements. If you already have a rabbit and are planning to buy more, you need to make sure that the pets can live together happily.

One of the most important criteria that need to be kept in mind is the space that you would provide the rabbits. The animals need the right amount of space to grow and develop.

These animals are known to be very active. You should be able to provide them a space where they can hop around without any constraints. There should be enough space for all the pets. If an animal has to compete with other animals for space, it will only lead to more trouble in the future.

The rabbits can get territorial and can fight with each other to establish their territory. You will have to keep a check on the pets to understand their basic behavior and their urge to establish a territory.

The rabbits can also grow fond of each other and live peacefully. Things will basically come down to the individual temperaments of the animals. You will have to devote some time to understanding it.

The age of the rabbits is another factor that should be taken into account. It is also known that if the rabbits are introduced to each other at a very young age, there is a chance that they will get along well.

It should be noted that you can keep a Netherland dwarf rabbit with other breeds of rabbits also, as long as there is space for everybody. An ideal scenario would be where you keep two to three rabbits. Remember to buy them at a young age so that they can grow together and bond well.

If you are looking to domesticate more than one Netherland dwarf rabbit, it is advised that you keep pairs of brothers and sisters. They will get along well. You can also keep pairs of males and females. As a rule, there should not be more than one male rabbit for two female rabbits.

Netherland dwarf rabbits and other pets

Netherland dwarf rabbits are social and loveable animals. You can expect your Netherland dwarf rabbit to be friendly towards other pets, but you will have to make sure that the pets are comfortable with each other.

If your Netherland dwarf rabbit is very young, you should make sure that you save him from bigger animals in the house that have a high prey drive. For example, a big cat might try to hunt the poor rabbit.

These animals might try to hurt the rabbit, and he would be too young to protect himself from any danger coming his way.

The type of pet is a very important criterion while determining whether the pets will get along or not. The Netherland dwarf rabbit will definitely get along with another sociable and friendly pet. If it finds the other animal a threat, then definitely they will not get along.

If you are very keen on keeping more than one kind of pet in the household, then it is better that the Netherland dwarf rabbit and the other pets are made to socialize right from a young age. This will help them to bond well with each other.

The lesser the space for the animals, the more difficult it will get for you to raise your pets. So, space is one factor that will always be important when you are hand raising your pets. You should always keep this in mind.

No matter how things are looking, you should always keep a close eye on your pets. Never commit the mistake of leaving them on their own. You might not realize but they can harm each other. The first few interactions need to be all the more monitored.

If you notice your pets are not getting along well with each other, it is important that you don't force them to interact. They should be allowed to interact and bond in a very natural way. In the case where the pets can't get along even after multiple tries, you should keep them away from each other so that no one is harmed in any way.

Chapter 3: Meeting the nutritional needs of the Netherland dwarf rabbit

Diet and habitat are the two most important requirements of any pet. You have to make sure that the pet gets a good diet and an appropriate habitat.

This chapter and the following chapter will help you to understand the dietary requirements and the habitat requirements of your pet animal.

1. Why is diet consideration so important?

Diet is the most important factor that contributes to the growth of an animal. If your Netherland dwarf rabbit is well fed, you will see the positive effects on his health, his mood and his general behavior. So, taking care of your pet's diet should be a priority for you.

The rabbit would naturally be inclined to eating grass and some kinds of shrubs, but you can slowly introduce new food types for your hand-raised pet. You can introduce him to various other kinds of foods. You also need to make sure that enough water is given to the animal.

If you take care of the dietary requirements of the Netherland dwarf rabbit, you automatically take care of many other aspects. If your pet is eating tasty and nutritious food, he will be healthy, disease free, stress free and happy.

So, it is important that you make all the efforts to make sure that the pet is getting his daily dose of nutrition and health. This is your responsibility as the owner of the pet.

Another important point when deciding and finally buying the various food types for your pet is that a pet is totally dependent on you for its needs. It won't be able to tell you that the food is good or bad in quality.

As a parent, it is your duty to make sure that the food is of the highest quality. You should avoid buying any low quality food just to save some money.

You will have to be very careful when you are planning the diet for your pet. A good diet will help to keep the pet animal healthy and will also protect him from various diseases.

First and foremost, you should always keep the surroundings of the Netherland dwarf rabbit clean and tidy. Your bunny will try to eat anything and everything around it. This will have a hazardous effect on his health.

You might find your pet eating the sofa covers or little toys. You should make sure that small toys and other toxic items are not kept around the animal. The health of the pet is your responsibility.

2. Nutritional needs of the Netherland dwarf rabbit

The Netherland dwarf rabbit needs a diet that is rich in protein and fiber. The rabbits need the high amounts of protein to supplement the growth of wool. You can see a decrease in the quantity and quality of wool in the Netherland dwarf rabbit that is not fed high amounts of protein and fiber.

Fiber is also good for the general digestion of the animal. Sometimes, the rabbit can swallow some hair by mistake. The fiber in the diet of the pet will help him to avoid any harmful consequences because of swallowing of the hair.

The food habits of captive bunnies vary slightly from wild bunnies. As the owner of the pet, you have to make sure that the pet gets to eat what he ate in his natural habitat. Along with that, other foods should also be introduced to him.

Grass and hay

It is known that grass and hay are the chief foods required for the rabbit. Alfalfa hay is known to have high amounts of fiber in it. The hay should be dry, but should also be soft. Soft and dry hay is the perfect meal for the rabbit. It is good for the gums of the animal and is also good for the digestive tract and stomach of the animal. A high amount of fiber in the diet is very important for a healthy digestive system.

You will have to watch for sharp pieces in the dried grass or hay. Such pieces will injure the pet. The sharp pieces can hurt the gums and inner lining of the mouth. If such pieces are swallowed, they can harm the digestive tract and the stomach of the pet.

Fresh fruit

The pet should be encouraged to eat fresh food. This is good for the digestive system of the pet and his health in general. Make sure that you don't serve him stale fruit. In fact, about ten per cent of the rabbit's diet should comprise of fresh fruits.

You can cut these fruits into small pieces before serving them to the rabbit, so that it is easier for the pet to chew. It should be noted that you should remove the seeds of the fruits before serving them to the rabbit.

You can include fruit such as apples, pears, apricots, bananas, cherries, star fruit, melon, plum, kiwi, papaya, mango, pineapple, berries, currants, peach and nectarines.

Vegetables

It is important to serve the rabbits fresh vegetables. You should be serving them one to two bowls of green leafy vegetables every single day. This will provide the rabbit with much-needed fiber along with other nutrients.

You should always try to keep the diet of the Netherland dwarf rabbit as natural as possible. You can include vegetables such as carrots, cabbage, bell peppers, celery, edible flowers, summer squash, Brussels sprouts, broccoli, zucchini and wheat grass.

Water

A Netherland dwarf rabbit needs good amounts of water for its survival. You should make sure that the animal always has access to drinking water.

Water helps the Netherland dwarf rabbit regulate its body temperature. The rabbit has a coat of fur over his body, and it is very important that the body of the pet maintains the right temperature.

If the Netherland dwarf rabbit is not hydrated well, he can develop severe health complications. You can even lose your pet Netherland dwarf rabbit because of a lack of water in his system. To avoid such things, make sure that the pet is hydrated at all times.

If you keep a water container in the hutch or cage of the pet Netherland dwarf rabbit, there is a high probability that the pet will play in the water. Even if he does not play, the water can spill easily in the cage or over the Netherland dwarf rabbit.

The water can wet the coat of the Netherland dwarf rabbit and it is important that the wool of the rabbit is always dry. The wet wool is the source of many health issues, especially skin-related diseases in the pet animal.

You should buy chew-proof water bottles for the Netherland dwarf rabbits. These bottles can be easily placed in the hutch or cage of the rabbit and are easily available.

It is easy to clean these water bottles. There are special brushes available in pet stores and also online that will allow you to clean the water bottles easily and without a fuss. Make sure that you clean them at least once a week.

You should also make sure that you purchase the right extensions to attach to the water bottle. These extensions will allow you to keep the water bottles in place and will also allow you to fix them at the right angle in the cage of the pet bunny.

If you stay at a place where water freezes during winters, you will have to take special care of the Netherland dwarf rabbit. You might be busy in your work and all the water in the water bottle could be frozen.

Such a condition can force the pet to go without water for extended periods, which is extremely dangerous for the Netherland dwarf rabbit. A simple solution to this problem is to use heated bowls in winter, but with this the same issue of the coat getting wet arises. To make things simpler, you need to check at regular intervals that the water is not frozen.

Commercial pellets

The diet of the rabbit should be highly nutritious. The food should contain a good amount of protein, fiber and other nutrients.

Even if you make sure that the rabbit is getting all its necessary nutrients from the food itself, you can't avoid the use of commercial pellets. At times, your bunny's diet might not be able to provide it with the right set of nutrients and vitamins.

There are many vitamin supplements that are available in tasty treat forms for the bunny. You should make sure that the commercial pellets have good amounts of both protein and fiber.

As a rule, you should make sure that the commercial pellets contain 10-15 per cent of protein in them. They should also have at least 18 per cent of fiber in them.

You should always consult a veterinarian before you administer any supplement to the rabbit. He will be the best judge of which supplements the rabbit requires and which ones he doesn't.

While it can be necessary to supplement certain vitamins and nutrients to the pet, you should also be aware of the hazards of over feeding a certain nutrient. If there is an overdose of a certain vitamin in the body of the rabbit, it can lead to toxicity.

The food that you feed the rabbit should have a good supply of nutrients, fiber and vitamins. The commercial pellets should only be used to supplement the diet of the pet and not to replace the diet.

You can easily buy the commercial pellets and other supplements online. You can also buy them from local feed stores and pet shops.

3. Foods to avoid

You should make it a rule never to feed anything to the Netherland dwarf rabbit, unless you are sure that it is good for the rabbit. In many cases, people feed them certain foods assuming that if humans can consume them, then rabbits can.

However, this is not true. There are many food types that are good for humans and many other animals but not suitable for your Netherland dwarf rabbit. You will jeopardize the health of the pet if you are not careful about what you serve to him.

Sometimes, the children of the house can force the pet animal to consume toxic and unhealthy food items just for fun. This can prove to be fatal for the rabbit.

It is important that you keep a check on what the kids are doing with the pet animal. It is always advised to let the children interact with the rabbit under an adult's supervision.

Keep the food of the rabbit fresh, simple and healthy. When you are giving fruit, you should make sure that it does not have seeds because the seeds can be poisonous for the pet rabbit.

If you are looking for a comprehensive list of food items that are unhealthy for the rabbit, then the given list will help you. You should avoid these food items:

- Caffeine
- Bread
- Citrus peels
- Corn
- Fresh peas
- Grains
- Green beans and legumes
- Rice
- Nuts
- Rhubarb leaves
- Seeds
- Sugar
- Beets
- Chocolates and cocoa beans
- Onion and potatoes
- Avocado
- Cookies, cakes and candy.

You can also contact the 'Pet poison control' authority is severe cases.

4. Treats

Treats are an essential part of a pet's meal plan. Treats are like small meal gifts that make the pet happy and delighted. The anticipation of getting a treat can also keep his behavior in check.

You should work on giving your pet high quality treats. The treat should be tasty but also nutritious. The Netherland dwarf rabbit should look forward to receiving a treat from you. This section will give you an idea of the kind of treats you can include in your rabbit's meal plan.

It should be noted that just because your Netherland dwarf rabbit seems to enjoy a treat, you can't give the food item to him all day long. You will have to keep a check on the amount of treats a pet will get. This is important because treats are not food replacements, they are only small rewards.

It is also important that the pet associates the treat with a reward. He should know that he is being served the treat reward for a reason. You should also make sure that the treats are healthy for the pet.

If you keep serving him the wrong kinds of treats, it will only affect his health in the long run. This is the last thing that you would want as a parent of the pet.

The treat should have the right mix of vitamins, fatty acids, minerals and proteins. This will make the treat healthy and wholesome. It is better if the treat has no sugar content. This is because the sugar will add no food value to the treat. Such healthy treats can be given to the pet on a daily basis without any issues.

Be careful if you are planning to give your pet a bowl of nuts or fruits as a treat. If you think that all fruits can serve as a treat for the pet, then you are absolutely wrong. Though a small amount of certain fruits should be fine, a larger quantity will affect the health of the pet. You should avoid nuts because they are toxic for the Netherland dwarf rabbit.

The pet can suffer from diarrhea and other gastro intestinal problems because of consuming large amount of toxic food. You will be shocked to know the problems that an undigested vegetable or fruit can cause in a Netherland dwarf rabbit.

If there is a piece of undigested food in the digestive tract of the animal, it can lead to obstructions and blockages. This will lead to many other digestive tract-related complications.

The bowel movements of the pet can be restricted or completely stopped because of the undigested food. This can even pose a very serious threat to the life of the animal.

You should also make sure that you peel and mash the items before you serve them to the animal. This will allow him to digest the food well. There have been many reports of blockages in rabbits because of undigested peels and seeds.

5. How much should you feed the Netherland dwarf rabbit?

As a new owner or a prospective owner, this is another concern that you must be having. It is recommended that you keep a bowl of food available for the pet at all times. If your pet is not well and the vet has advised you to feed him less, then you can alter the quantities of food items that you serve him.

There are many owners who decrease the quantity of food they feed the pet animal if he happens to gain some weight. You are advised not to do so. This can be detrimental for the health of the pet.

If your Netherland dwarf rabbit has gained some weight, you should focus on increasing the amount of activity that he gets. Don't deprive him of his food. This will have a negative effect on the health of the Netherland dwarf rabbit.

Good exercise and food high in protein and fiber are enough for the Netherland dwarf rabbit to lose weight and remain healthy. You can also expect a relatively younger Netherland dwarf rabbit to eat more than the adults.

It is said that one of the first signs of health issues in a Netherland dwarf rabbit is a change in his appetite. You should always keep an eye on whether the pet is eating well or not.

A simple way to keep track of the Netherland dwarf rabbit's diet is to check his food bowl after every meal he has. If you see any abrupt change in his food habits, you should consult the doctor. It is always better to catch a health problem in the earliest stages.

6. Introducing new foods to the Netherland dwarf rabbits

If you want to introduce new foods or switch foods, you can't suddenly change the rabbit's usual meal plan. This will put the bunny off. He might even give up eating altogether. This is something that you would never want.

The Netherland dwarf rabbit will naturally be inclined to eat hay and grass. You should also introduce him to certain vegetables and fruit. This will have a very positive effect on his overall health.

It is suggested that the pet should be introduced to different food types quite early in his life. This will make it easier for you and also for the pet Netherland dwarf rabbit. This will help the bunny to have his preferences and will also make things easier for you.

If you don't introduce new foods to the pet Netherland dwarf rabbit, he will turn out to be a very fussy eater. In addition, you will find it very difficult to provide him with the right types of food.

You should slowly introduce new foods to the pet. There are some simple tips and tricks that you should be following to make sure that the pet is eating well even when new foods are being introduced.

You should introduce one new food at a time. A simple way of introducing new food in the diet of the Netherland dwarf rabbit is by starting out with a small amount of the food. Take a bowl and add the usual food of the pet in it. Now, take a very small amount of the new food that you wish to feed your pet in the bowl. Mix the contents and serve the food to the pet animal.

You should remember that the rabbit needs time to get used to it. There is nothing to worry about even if the pet leaves the new food in the beginning. Just keep adding a very small amount of the food item to the usual food of the pet. This might take some time so be prepared. Once you see that the pet has started eating the new food along with the usual old food, you can gradually increase the portion of the new food.

Chapter 4: Habitat requirements

If you can't provide your pet a habitat that keeps him happy and safe, then you will fail as the owner of the pet. You need to make sure that the pet gets what would make it happy and comfortable. The animal can slip into sadness and depression if his habitat requirements are not met.

Pets require a proper shelter so that you can keep them safe from the changes in weather and also from possible attacks from predators. It is advisable that you make the necessary arrangements for your pet before you bring him home so that you can get them straight into their shelter when they are home.

1. Building a good shelter

Proper shelters are extremely important for your pet. When the weather is not suitable, or if the pet is unwell or if the animal wants to simply rest, having good housing is a must.

Construction

The construction should ensure that there are no projections on the surface of the cage or shelter to prevent injury. You must clean all the exposed surfaces and disinfect them to ensure the good health of your pet.

If you are using treated wood or any paint on the surface of the construction material, it should not be toxic to the Netherland dwarf rabbit.

Wooden material requires preservatives to prevent any chance of rotting or warping. The flooring should be leveled as much as possible and must not be slippery. Good drainage is necessary to make sure that any waste is drained out.

The doors should be wide enough for the Netherland dwarf rabbit. The height should be such that the rabbit does not hurt himself while playing. Use bolts on the top and bottom to make sure that the door is fastened well when the Netherland dwarf rabbit is inside.

You can even have a top door that can be secured when in the open position. The disadvantage with a top door is that ventilation and sunlight is reduced when it is closed.

The shelter should also have good lighting to ensure that the Netherland dwarf rabbit can see properly. The keeper should be able to examine the animal and handle it safely.

You can have portable lighting as well. If you do plan to install the lighting inside the shelter, make sure that the bulbs are out of the rabbit's reach. The cabling should be secure and of high quality to prevent any chance of fires or short circuits.

The air circulation should be adequate while ensuring that there are no drafts inside the shelter. You can even install safety glass with each window to keep the shelter warm. It is best to keep one window open at all times unless the temperature drops drastically.

If you do not provide enough ventilation, there are chances that your Netherland dwarf rabbit will develop respiratory issues. While airflow should be kept at a maximum, you need to keep a constant check on the dust that is entering the shelter.

Ideally the size of the shelter should be large enough to allow the rabbit to rise easily, turn around while inside the shelter and also maintain a safe distance from the other rabbits that you may have housed inside the shelter. If you have a large space that houses many pets, space for each pet should be the top priority.

Safety

A shelter should be able to keep the pet animal safe. He should be safe from predators and also from hazards such as fire. You will have to take into consideration all the fire safety recommendations that are laid out by your local government.

If you are unsure, you can also seek advice from a Fire Prevention Officer in your locality to understand the statutory requirements. If you have any combustible liquid or material in the area surrounding the shelter, it should be removed instantly. You should also make sure that you do not smoke in the shelter area or in the areas near it.

The fire extinguishers, alarm systems and other equipment should be checked on a regular basis by someone who is qualified. If you have any electrical installation in the shelter, it should be periodically inspected and maintained. The fittings and wires should not be accessible to the pets.

You must also make sure that it is earthed properly and is kept safe from any rodent. If you need to use extension cables and leads, you should make sure that it does not get entangled in the legs of the animal, leading to serious injuries.

Metal pipe work and any steel that is used in the structure should be earthed well. You can take additional precautions by ensuring that all the installations are protected by an RCD or a residual current device.

Lastly, in case there is an outbreak of a fire, you should make sure that your pet animal or animals can be released easily. A fire exit should be installed and an emergency turnout procedure should be planned and communicated to everyone who is working with the pets. This is necessary when you are housing large number of pets in a designated area.

2. Types of shelters

The habitat should be spacious, comfortable and safe for the pet. The pet should feel at home in the habitat that you provide it. You should try to furnish the enclosure in a way that the cage resembles the natural habitat of the rabbit. This will keep him happy and upbeat, which is essential for his overall well being.

If you are looking for shelter ideas for your pet Netherland dwarf rabbit, then you would be happy to know that you have many options. This section will explore the various shelter ideas for a Netherland dwarf rabbit.

The pet is more like a new member of the family, a new baby in the house. So when you buy the animal, you should make sure that you understand the needs of the animal at various stages of his life. It is better to spend some extra money in the beginning than to see your pet being sad and lonely in the shelter. You should make sure that you understand this before you finalize a cage for the pet.

Building the ideal cage

You can buy or build a cage for your pet rabbit. It is very important to design and build the right enclosure for the rabbit. The enclosure will be like a home to the rabbit, so it is very important that the enclosure meets all the requirements of the rabbit.

A good amount of enclosure space is essential when designing and planning the cage. This is because the pet rabbit needs some space to move around. The cage should not feel like a prison. It has to be safe and secure.

The ideal cage of the rabbit should be 18 x 24 x 18 inches. These dimensions of the enclosure are the minimum requirements of the Netherland dwarf rabbit. It is advised to keep the size six times the size of the Netherland dwarf rabbit.

There might be an instance when you would have to isolate your Netherland dwarf rabbit. Your habitat should allow you to do so. The isolation could be needed due to some disease or infection that the animal could be suffering from.

The isolated area would help the animal to be treated well. This will also help in keeping the other pets in the house safe.

A simple trick that you can use to make the animal comfortable with the cage is to instruct the bunny to go inside the cage, but leave the door of the cage open. If you do this, the Netherland dwarf rabbit will also not feel captive.

Let the rabbit come out and go inside the cage at will, but make sure that it spends considerable time in the cage. It is important that the pet is not forced to go into the cage. He should find the cage homely and should go there without a hesitation.

If you are unable to supervise the pet for some reason, don't make the mistake of keeping the cage door open. You should keep the cage door closed so that the pet stays inside. This is to avoid any unpleasant incidents.

You should always remember that no matter how much you train the rabbit, you can be surprised and shocked by him. He is a playful, chirpy and active animal and will not miss any chance to do some mischief.

It is extremely important that you clean the cage regularly. A dirty cage will only lead to infections for the pet and also other pets. You should clean the cage daily and should change the food and water provided for him.

The outdoor enclosure should be planned and constructed keeping in mind the basic nature of the rabbit. The animal should have fun, but should also be safe and should not get any opportunity to run away from the enclosure.

The enclosure needs to be constructed with high quality material. The outer area of your garden and backyard should also be covered. You can look at using the using the chain links that are utilized to build cyclone fences. These fences are very strong and durable.

There is a chance that while playing the rabbit's head might just get stuck in a gap in the fence. To prevent any such accident, you can install a preventive wire outside the main fence. This will ensure that the rabbit does not get trapped when you are not around.

You have to take preventive measures so that the Netherland dwarf rabbit does not climb out. You should make sure that the enclosure has fencing on the top area. The rabbit also loves digging. It should also be taken care of that the rabbit can't dig and eventually escape the enclosure.

The enclosure should be safe and also well fenced. This will make sure that the rabbit can't escape. To make things look like his natural habitat, cover the floor with sand, plants, wooden chips and twigs. Your house should have fencing to protect the pet animal from stray animals. The pet should be able to be at peace when in the enclosure. He should be able to do whatever he wants.

Rabbit hutch

A rabbit hutch can be defined as a cage for the rabbit that is constructed generally with wood and a wire mesh that surrounds it. Most rabbit hutches have long legs to keep them anywhere. The ones without legs can be placed over tables or other safe surfaces.

Building a rabbit hutch is one of the most popular choices. You should make sure that you have the provisions to build it in your house. You can keep one in the backyard, basement or any other area of the house.

It is important that you understand that a rabbit hutch is only one option that you have when your pet needs to be kept in a cage like environment. This does not mean that you keep the pet in the hutch and forget about him.

The hutch needs to be easily accessible to you or a family member. You should check on the rabbit from time to time. You should also allow the pet some time outside the hutch to just walk around.

Many cases have been reported in the past where the owners' negligence towards the Netherland dwarf rabbits caused serious issues in the animals, such as stress and depression. You can't abandon your rabbit in a comfortable hutch. The pet should be kept indoors as much as possible. The hutch can be used when you are not around to care for the pet.

You can buy the rabbit hutch or can design it yourself. It is important that it meets all the requirements of the pet animal. To begin with, the hutch needs to be spacious. The animal should have enough space to walk around.

You should make sure that the rabbit hutch does not suffocate the rabbit. It should be airy and well ventilated. You should make sure that the rabbit has access to food and water in the rabbit hutch. You can install a feed hopper and a good watering system in the rabbit hutch to ensure the same.

You should also try to make the hutch attractive for the rabbit. He should not feel bored and suffocated in there. The hutch should feel like a fun home for him. There are some simple ways in which you can make the hutch a lively place for the rabbit.

Keep some small and interesting toys for the Netherland dwarf rabbit in the hutch. You should make sure that the toys don't scare the pet away. They should be inviting and fun for him. This will keep him happy and entertained.

The rabbit hutch should allow proper sanitation. Many cases of diseases have been reported in Netherland dwarf rabbits due to improper sanitation.

The rabbit's hutch would need to be cleaned regularly to make sure that there are no disease carrying bacteria and viruses in there. These are simple things, but critical when it comes to the well being of the pet in the long run.

The nest boxes that are used for the kits should be sanitized regularly. They should be stored safely and properly when not in use. You can store them and use them for the next set of kits that you might have.

If you are planning to keep more than one Netherland dwarf rabbit, then you can work on giving them a common habitat. Some people would choose to give separate shelters to the animals. The idea of providing separate shelters is also fine.

If the pets get along, then they can be kept in a common cage. However, in case the rabbits are not getting along, keeping them in a common cage will only lead to more problems in the future, so this should be avoided.

If you are planning on domesticating more than one rabbit, you can consider buying another cage. This cage could be very simple and basic. The main purpose of this extra cage is to use it when one of the rabbits is sick. The cage will help you to isolate the sick pet animal.

A vet will always advise you to isolate a sick pet. This is necessary so that the pet can recover nicely in the absence of other pets. He would need some space to himself. What is also important is that he should not transmit the disease to the healthy pets. The isolation helps to avoid such a situation.

3. Accessories

When you bring a pet home, the pet will be scared of the new surroundings. You will have to make all the attempts that will help the pet to adjust in the new environment.

When you are planning the furnishing and accessories of the shelter, you should make sure that you give the pet an environment that closely resembles his natural habitat. This will keep him happy and spirited.

Besides the basic stuff such as food and water, it is also important to accessorize the cage well. This is important because the right accessories will help him to feel like he is at home. They will bring him closer to his natural habitat and natural tendencies.

There are several accessories available these days that will help you to keep your pet happy. If you go to a pet toyshop, you will get many ideas for the accessories that you can keep in the cage of the pet.

Bedding

Keeping your pets warm is very important. For this, adequate bedding material is necessary. This not only provides warmth but also protects the animal against any chance of injury. When the Netherland dwarf rabbit lies down on the floor, he will be comfortable with good bedding.

The bedding material should be free from mold and too much dust. The material should also be non-toxic to a Netherland dwarf rabbit. The best option is matting, as it is also absorbent by nature.

You can even add material like straw, shavings and other material that can absorb any urine. This should be changed regularly and well managed to ensure complete hygiene and disease prevention.

There are many types of bedding available these days that can help your pet to have rest and fun when he wants. For example, you can get bedding in the shape of a cave. This will be fun for the pet. The right kind of bedding provided for the rabbit is a simple way of keeping the pet animal comfortable and stress-free.

There are cage liners easily available on the market. You can use these to line the bottom of the cage. They are easy to attach and detach, so are very popular amongst owners.

It is also important that the cage is deep for this type of setting. The liners should be made from a good quality fabric. These liners are safe for the pet because they don't have sharp pieces that can hurt him.

It is easier for the pet to walk on these liners. Fabric liners are actually considered the best option for a bunny's cage. One disadvantage of these liners would be that the pet will try to dig into them and might also spill his food and water. It can be inconvenient to the pet-parent at such a time.

Another popular choice of bedding for the cage is wood shavings. It is important that the shavings are free from phenol. It is also important that the cage is deep, otherwise the shavings will just fall off.

The pet can safely dig in these wood shavings. He can have his fun in this simple way. The wood shavings are relatively odorless because they allow air amongst the shavings.

The wood shavings also have some disadvantages. The shavings will keep falling in the eyes of the pet or they might fall in the water or food containers.

You can use aspen shavings. They are considered the safest of all. The second choice of shavings could be kiln dried pine shavings. You should not use untreated pine shavings or cedar shavings. These can be harmful for the pet.

If you can't install liners in the cage of the Netherland dwarf rabbit, then paper shavings is your second best option. They look quite similar to the wood shavings.

One downside of this kind of bedding is that the paper bedding is very dusty in nature. This might lead to dry skin in your Netherland dwarf rabbit. If your pet already has dry skin, the condition might be aggravated.

Rugs and blankets

You can also keep a couple of warm blankets inside the cage. The bunny will play and will also bite them. The rabbit will also like snuggling into the blanket. You should try to make the cage as comfortable as possible, so that the pet animal does not feel like a captive and starts liking the cage.

If the Netherland dwarf rabbit is old, clipped or is injured, you have to keep him protected from any draft or low temperature. You can also use these rugs to keep flies at bay. Any turnout rug should be removed in case the weather improves to prevent the cage from getting very warm.

The size of the rug should be good enough to suit the size of the bunny. You need the right size to ensure that there are no abrasions, hair loss or restricted movements. They should be removed on a regular basis to check the body condition of the pet. You should also make sure that the bunny does not get too hot because of the rug being on him constantly.

The rugs should be cleaned and repaired regularly. In case of any wetness in the rugs, you should have a spare one that you can use on your pet animal. These precautions ensure that the animal stays clear of any illnesses.

Containers for food and water

It is also extremely important that you give due importance to the containers that would be used to serve food and water to the Netherland dwarf rabbits. What makes this important is the fact that dirty containers are carriers of allergies and diseases. These allergies and diseases can further turn into serious issues if not treated well.

The containers should also be sturdy enough to hold all the food and water. They should also allow the pet to feed himself without any difficulty. So, even if you have not thought of selecting containers as an important step in animal care, you can do so now.

The food containers should be of good quality and should ideally be made of aluminum or good grade plastic. A poor quality container will only contribute towards spoiling the food, which is something you will never want. The spoilt food is not just a hassle for you, but is also harmful to the health of your bunny.

A water container has some limitations. It can lead to wet coat for the rabbit, which in turn can lead to many water borne diseases. You can use specialized water bottles to keep water for the rabbit in the cage.

If you are concerned about the soiling of the food or if you have more than one pet that would eat from the same food container, then a hayrack could be your ideal buy. A trough or pellet bin with hayracks will help you to avoid the soiling of food items.

The container would also allow more than one animal to eat from the same container. You should choose a size that is most ideal for you. Each animal should get enough space to eat comfortably.

The containers should be washed with good quality soap powder at least twice a week. It is very important that the containers are kept clean at all times. Do not forget to remove the leftover food or dirty water from the containers.

There are many different kinds of feeders available today. You should go for a feeder that suits your needs the best.

Toys

You also have to make sure that the pet is entertained. The pet can get bored easily, which will make him a little aggressive. To keep him occupied, you can keep various kinds of toys in the pet's cage.

The right kind of toys should be bought for the pets. You will get many ideas when you visit a shop that keeps toys for rabbits, but it is important that the toys are of good quality. They should not be harmful for the pet.

It is better if the toys are washable. This will enable you to wash the pet's toys every now and then when they are dirty. The harmful bacteria will also be removed from the toys when they are washed.

In addition, make sure that the toys can't be shredded by the animal. If the pet is able to shred the toy, he will swallow the shreds. This is very harmful and will only invite more trouble for the pet. To avoid all these issues, buy the right kind of toys.

You should remember that the furnishing should also be designed keeping in mind the comfort and also the security of the pet. The furnishing should not in any way disturb the lifestyle of the rabbit. It should gel with the personality of the animal.

A simple way to keep the rabbit happy is to give him an old t-shirt or piece of cloth. The pet will love it. He will act as if he is digging in the t-shirt. He will also try to fit in the t-shirt. This will keep him busy and happy.

4. Cleaning the habitat

The pet can't clean the cage on its own, and if it is forced to stay in an unhygienic environment, he will fall sick. It is extremely important to clean the cage of the pet. You will not necessarily enjoy this process, but still you have to do it.

The first thing you need to make sure is that the housing area is properly sanitized. Building the housing area on an elevated area is one of the best measures to keep it from having any build-up of moisture.

There are certain tasks that you need to do daily, while several others need to be done once a week. Similarly, if the food and water containers look dirty, they should be cleaned and refilled. It is best that you clean out the feeding and water containers on a daily basis.

The food and water must be replaced to prevent the bunny from eating any rotten or spoiled food. It is important that the cage is free from all bacteria and virus that are known to cause diseases in pet animals. You should keep some time designated for the cleaning of the cage.

At least once a week, the litter and the bedding material should be changed. In case you notice any dampness in the bedding, it needs to be changed immediately. Damp areas encourage the growth of fungi. They are the primary cause for respiratory issues and skin troubles in bunnies.

To clean the shelter thoroughly, you have to start by dusting and dry cleaning. You will have to sweep the floor of the coop and dust off the ceiling.

All the fixtures, nest boxes, air inlets and fans must be dusted. The feed from the feeders should be removed. Any feces and debris is scraped off the floor and the perches. You can even vacuum the floor as an option.

The power should be turned off before you wet clean the cage. There are some basic steps that you need to follow each time you clean the cage.

Any area that is heavily soiled can be soaked with a low-pressure sprayer. Until the manure and dirt is softened, keep it soaked so you can remove it easily.

All the surfaces in the shelter should be cleaned out fully. Focus on the ceiling trusses, the wall sills, the windowsills and any area where dust may accumulate. Use a mild detergent with pH that ranges between 6 and 8. A mild alkali solution like baking soda solution can be sprayed around to disinfect the shelter thoroughly.

Rinsing the soap off completely before you allow it to dry is a good idea. Use plain water to rinse and make sure that there aren't any puddles left behind in the shelter.

The shelter can be allowed to dry by air-drying the building. All the windows and vents should be opened. It is a good idea to use a fan or a blower if possible. The best option is to clean when the weather is warm and sunny. This improves the drying process.

Any repairs in the area should be made before you disinfect the shelter one final time. The rodent holes should be sealed, lighting fixtures must be repaired and any breakages or protruding areas in the construction must be repaired.

The most crucial step is the final disinfecting, which is usually overlooked by those who have a small hutch or cage. Once the whole shelter has been washed, rinsed and dried, you should use a good disinfectant.

Your veterinarian will be able to provide you with spray or fumigation options. The best option with most small shelters is to use a mild spray to disinfect it.

Make sure you follow the instructions provided by the manufacturer with respect to diluting the disinfectant. Usually you will need about one gallon of the diluted disinfectant per 200 square feet of space of the shelter.

Another point that you need to understand is that you should not use very strong disinfectants. Such products can be very harmful if they are ingested even in the smallest of quantities.

You should always look for mild ant bacterial soaps and detergents to clean the vessels and the floor.

If you want the process to be more thorough, you can even soak all the feeders and the bowls in 200-ppm chlorine solution. You can make that by mixing 1 tablespoon of chlorine bleach in a gallon of boiling water. With these steps, you should be able to raise a pet that is in the best of its health.

Chapter 5: Proofing the house

You should know that a pet left on his own has a tendency to injure himself. If you don't pay attention, the damage could be very serious and irrevocable. A solution to keep your pet safe is to proof your home. This chapter will discuss the potential dangers to the Netherland dwarf rabbit and also some simple ways to proof your house. This will help you to save things from the Netherland dwarf rabbit and also to save the Netherland dwarf rabbit from potential dangers.

1. Bunny proofing the house

A Netherland dwarf rabbit has a very curious personality. He will not think twice before charging into unknown territory. You might be busy with some work, and before you know it your pet might be walking into some real danger.

When you have a Netherland dwarf rabbit at home, you have to ensure that the pet is safe at all times. The rabbit is so tiny that you might not know where he is most of the time. This makes it very important that you understand the behavior of your pet very well.

There is no use crying after the damage has been done. It is always better to take the necessary precautions in the very beginning.

To begin with, you should make sure that all kind of medicines, syrups, chemicals and tablets are out of reach of the pet. These can be very harmful for the pet. You can also get childproof cabinets in your home to keep all such potentially dangerous products in those cabinets.

You should make sure that the pet sleeps in his cage. This is for his safety and also for the good of the family members. You can also keep him in the cage when you can't supervise him and his actions.

Keep the waste bin and waste stuff away from him because he might try to play with things that could be harmful for him. This might be very difficult for you in the beginning to look into areas and places that have hidden dangers for the pet.

However, you will definitely learn with time and experience. You should make sure there are no sharp edges on your furniture that could hurt the animal.

You must also keep the toilet door closed to make sure that he does not enter the toilet. If there are any areas of the house that the pet needs to keep away from, you have to keep them closed and blocked. If you don't do so, the pet can just enter the space when you are not around.

The Netherland dwarf rabbit can slip inside a toilet seat, a bucket of water or a sink and can get himself killed. To avert any such incident, make sure that these areas are out of his reach.

The Netherland dwarf rabbit might accidentally swallow the small or shredded pieces of toys. Make sure that the toys that you allow the pet to play with are of good quality. They need to be sturdy and safe, and they should be impossible to swallow for the Netherland dwarf rabbit.

As you know Netherland dwarf rabbits are very small in size. If somebody sits on him accidentally or uses a reclining chair when he is inside, the consequences can be fatal. To be on the safer side, always check the chair or sofa that you are about to sit on. You don't want to sit on your pet and injure him.

The pet should stay away from the plants of the house. You should also make sure that he stays away from Styrofoam products. All kinds of sponges should not be in the reach of the Netherland dwarf rabbit. The pet animal could bite into them and swallow them. This can be potentially dangerous.

Rubber items can also be very dangerous if they are swallowed by the pet. Keep away all rubber products so that the pet can't reach them. This includes both soft rubber and foam rubber products.

You should make sure that the pet stays away from stacks of clothes. Keep the cupboards locked and keep the laundry area closed and locked. If the Netherland dwarf rabbit gets inside a stack of clothes, you will have a very hard time finding him.

Don't keep breakable pieces in the reach of the pet. The pet will approach it and might destroy it or hurt himself. There are certain food items that are very dangerous for the bunny. You should make sure that the pet has no access to these items.

All the electrical equipment should be kept at a safe distance from the pet. The sockets should be covered so that the pet animal is not harmed. You should not leave any food items on the table or shelves. He might eat it, without knowing whether it is good or bad for him.

Creating such an environment is essential to the Netherland dwarf rabbit and also to the other family members. If you wish to make your home suitable for the Netherland dwarf rabbit then you should be ready to let off certain things. You should not keep expensive carpets in areas where the pet will play because the rabbit will spoil it. Instead, make use of old rags and carpets.

If your pet Netherland dwarf rabbit swallows something toxic for him, you might not even get a chance to take him to the veterinarian and save him. The digestive system of the animal is such that blockages can happen easily and they can be very dangerous. There are many rabbits that lose their lives because of such blockages.

This makes it very important to look for areas of hidden dangers and keep the pet safe. The Netherland dwarf will try to chew anything it can. It will chew on rubber items, though such things are very harmful for him. It is you who needs to make sure that the pet does not chew on the wrong items.

2. Fencing

As a rabbit owner, you should also understand the importance of fencing the habitat of the rabbit. If the rabbit is kept in a cage that is kept inside the house at all times, then you can skip the need to fence. However, if you plan to leave the rabbit in an open space for longer durations, fencing is a must.

Fencing is also good for owners that have more than one rabbit. You could keep your rabbits in the open for longer durations of time without the fear of them being attacked. The rabbits could play and keep themselves entertained in the open spaces.

Fencing is a fundamental requirement when you keep your rabbit in your backyard or in an open land surrounded by wild animals. There have been many incidents with many rabbit owners where their rabbits have been attacked by wild animals.

If you have a pet, it can be extremely disturbing to find out that your beloved pet animal has been killed or taken away by predators. If you have a large number of rabbits on a farm for showing or other commercial purposes, this is definitely a huge economic loss.

It is important that the fencing is sturdy and well planned. A big animal such as a fox or dog can get over a fence that is about 5 feet in height. You will have to choose an enclosure based on the kind of predators that you are trying to ward off.

Preventing predators

The common predators that can pose danger to your pet rabbit or rabbits are dogs, foxes, badgers and cats. It is also known that weasels, snakes, ferrets and raccoons can act as deadly predators for the rabbits.

If you live in a place that is inhabited by any of these animals then you will face the issue of keeping the predator away. You should never underestimate a predator like a fox. Though they look and are perceived to be similar to dogs, they can climb over a fence or just jump over it very easily if they want to get to your rabbit. The options that you have with respect to fences to prevent predators are as follows:

Electric netting: This is an ideal type of fencing provided there is no chance of a short circuit because of long grass. You must also avoid this fencing in areas that have children playing in it. If your area is suitable for electric netting, it is the best option as it is portable and can be move to areas where the rabbit has access to fresh grass.

Triple wire fencing: This is a secure form of low fencing that can also include an electrical wire at the base. This will prevent any digging and will stop predators that will climb over it as well.

Improving security

If your area has foxes as the main predators, the fence should be buried deep into the ground to make sure that digging is not an option. It will also need to be tall enough to prevent the predator from climbing over.

There are several quality grades for the wiring. Getting strong netting will also ensure that the predator cannot tear through the fence. If you notice that the predator is trying to tear through the fence, it is a good idea to double it up to the height that the predator can tear through.

A large fox can be kept out if your fence is about 6 feet in height. Turning the top upwards and running an electric strand on top will also help prevent any climbing. Make sure that the electric strand is high enough to keep children from reaching it. In places that have a high incidence of fox attacks, a fence that is less than 5 meters is not recommended.

Foxes are known to dig through areas where the ground is soft. Badgers are also extremely good at digging and tearing the net apart. If this is the primary issue that you are facing, it is a good idea to have the fencing buried up to about 8 inches into the ground.

Areas with clay soil are not susceptible to digging. On the other hand, if you have sandy soil, you will have to bury the fence as deep as you can. You should remember that any ground that humans can dig into easily will be easy for foxes and badgers.

You can even turn the fence up after 8 inches of burying it. Covering the turned up area with rubble and bricks is a great idea. Additionally, you can even cover the wire with soil after it has been dug in.

If badgers are the primary predator, overlaying the fence with an extra layer of netting or having triple wire is a good idea. This will ensure that strong predators like badgers stay out. Adding an electric wire at the height of the nose of the badger will also help immensely.

Patching the fence up with gravel boards at the bottom is also a good idea. This means that the predator will have to dig deeper to get through. You can also turn the wire out. You may have to peg the wire down after laying the wire on the surface of the ground for about 24 inches.

The action of the earthworms will help the fence sink in deeper. You will also notice that the grass will grow through the wire.

Netting options

Chicken netting is quite useful to protect an enclosed area. This type of netting is also called rabbit wire as it is used to keep rabbits from digging through and getting to crops. This net can keep off predators such as dogs and foxes.

There are various grades of chicken netting. Across the widest part of the gap or hole in the fence, the netting is about 50mm. These wires are galvanized to make sure that they do not rust.

You can get cheaper nets that are 2, 3, 4 and 6 feet in width or about 10, 25 and 50 meters lengthwise. If the predator in your area is a fox, you will need to get netting that will allow you to dig it in at least up to 18 inches while allowing ample height to prevent the predator from getting in.

Agricultural merchants will be able to sell chicken netting to you. You will also be able to find several suppliers online. Buying online is a cheaper option most of the time as there are regular deals and offers for you to look out for.

If you don't have foxes in your area, you can also opt for portable netting. These nets are meant to keep various pets in a specific area and are not used for predators. This is ideal even when you want to restrain the rabbit when you are introducing a new pet in the household.

Fencing a large area

If you have a large area that you have to enclose, a low electric fence is a good idea. With most predators, the first step is for them to investigate the fence to look for the easiest way in. While doing this, if the electric fence even touches their nose, they will not attempt to get close to it.

You also have the option of sheep or pig fencing. This can be installed by a contractor. Although these fences are lower, the option of adding electrical wires makes it the most economical option available to you. The only thing you need to make sure is that the grass does not cut the electric connection, rendering it ineffective.

Of course, fencing is the first step to protecting your pet. You must also make sure that you keep the pet inside the housing area every night. This housing must be locked to keep the pet additionally secure. If you are unable to lock the housing area each night, getting an automatic door closer is a good idea, as it can be timed as per your convenience.

Chapter 6: Maintaining health of the Netherland dwarf rabbit

It is very important that you invest your time and energy in understanding the health requirements of the rabbit. This will allow your pet rabbit to enjoy a happier and healthier life.

There are a few diseases to which a Netherland dwarf rabbit is susceptible. An understanding of the symptoms and precautions of these diseases will help you to avoid them.

It should be understood that sometimes a rabbit can suffer for a very long time from a particular disease. This will make it very difficult to treat him later. No symptom should be ignored. You should take the pet animal to a veterinarian even at the slightest doubt.

This chapter will help you to understand how you can keep your pet healthy. You will be able to understand the symptoms, precautions and cure of common diseases that can affect your pet animal.

1. Understanding symptoms at an early stage

It is a known fact that the earlier you catch the symptoms of a disease, the higher the chances are to treat it. Often many symptoms go unnoticed, leading to serious complications and issues in the future for the pet.

The first way to catch symptoms at an early stage is to spending quality time with the pet. This will allow you to understand the mannerisms and behavior of your pet in a better light. Even the slightest deviation from this usual behavior should be taken as a warning signal.

Rabbits all over the world are susceptible to various diseases. Some of these diseases are more common than others, and most of them can be very dangerous if necessary precautions are not taken.

It should be noted that even if your pet is healthy and all seems to be just fine with him, you should make sure that you take him to the vet for periodic visits.

The vet will examine the health of the pet rabbit and will help you to understand if something needs your attention. As with humans, an early detected problem or disease can be treated easily in pets.

There are a few symptoms that will help you to identify stress and sickness in your pet. Examine the behavior and the body of the pet carefully.

You should never ignore any symptom that you see because an ignored symptom will lead to serious problems later.

The following signs can help you to understand that there is something wrong with the pet rabbit:

- **Respiratory**: You should pay attention to the breathing of the pet animal. If the pet is having difficulty breathing, this could be an obvious symptom of some disease.

- **Nose**: The sick pet could be snoring very loudly while making noises from is nose. There could be some discharge from the nose.

- **Eating disorders**: He will lose his appetite. The pet will lose an interest in eating and drinking. This is a signal that something is definitely wrong with the pet. If the animal is not treated on time, you will see that his appetite decreases with time. It will decrease to a point that it will become difficult for the animal to carry on his daily tasks. The rabbit could also show the symptom of diarrhea. He will suffer from frequent and liquid stools.

- **Mobility**: A sick rabbit will appear as if he is out of balance. He will be fidgety in his movements. In some cases, the rabbit might not even have the strength to walk.

- **Coat of the animal**: A dull coat is also an indication of a sick pet. The quality of the fur or the coat directly represents the health of the pet. If the pet is losing too much hair, even that could be an indication.

- **Eyes**: The eyes could be swollen or have discharge.

- **Ears**: The ears could be swollen or could have visibly drooped.

As soon as you spot any of the symptoms, take the pet rabbit to a qualified and good veterinarian. He/she will be able to confirm the presence of disease and stress in the animal.

If you find your pet behaving different from normal, then the first step you should take is to provide him warmth. It is important that the pet is not cold and that proper temperature is maintained.

You should try to make the pet feel secure and safe when he is stressed. You should keep him securely on a comfortable blanket to make him feel easy and comfortable.

You should make sure that your pet can rest well in a calm environment. Keep him away from other animals. Make sure that there are no noises around the rabbit. Discourage your family members from gathering around the pet. This will stress him more.

It is important that you are able to identify the signs of emergency in your pet so that you can act without delay.

2. How to prevent diseases

While you are learning about the various diseases, their symptoms and cure, it is also important to learn about simple ways to prevent disease.

You should make sure that your pet is always kept in a clean environment. A neat and clean environment will help you to ward off many common ailments and diseases.

The food that the animal eats, the conditions around him the care and love that you give him will all affect the general well being and the health of the rabbit.

You should also make sure that the pet is well fed at all times. Low quality food and insufficient food can also lead to health-related issues in the pet.

There are many issues that might not start as a big problem, but become serious problems if not treated on time. If you can detect a disease at an early stage, there are more chances that the disease will be cured.

Apart from this, you should take him for regular check-ups to the veterinarian. You should always consult a veterinarian when you find any unusual traits and symptoms in the pet.

It is important to control and prevent diseases in your pet animal. The pet should be examined completely before you buy them from the breeder. Make sure that you only opt for reliable sources when it comes to breeders. This is a simple way to ensure that your pet starts out healthy. Such a pet has stronger chances to overcome various diseases.

Make sure that your pet has access to regular vaccinations and medicines. You must always give them medicines and vaccinations only after you have consulted a veterinarian. You should never experiment with their health. Wrong medication can lead to serious issues.

If you find a pet unwell, make sure that you isolate him immediately. This should be done until the condition improves because there is no way of knowing if it can harm your other pets in any way. This will help to keep the other pets safe and disease free.

In case of any death, ensure that the rabbit that is dead is incinerated or buried properly. It is also recommended that you get a diagnostic report at the earliest. The samples from the carcass can be sent to the vet to determine the cause of the rabbit's death.

If you have visitors in your house regularly, make sure that they do not meet the sick rabbit without any protective clothing. This is to help the rabbit get better and also to avoid making these people carriers of disease.

Taking some precautions can help you save a lot of money that you may have to spend on medical bills and veterinarian services otherwise. This is important so that even the smallest health issue can be tracked at an early stage. Prevention is always better than cure.

Veterinary care

If you wish to keep your Netherland dwarf rabbit happy and healthy, you need specialized veterinary care to do so. While a regular vet will be able to provide you with temporary relief during an emergency, you will need a qualified veterinarian that practices medicine on rabbits.

You need to find a veterinarian that understands your concern for your pet rabbit. So, when you are in talks with a vet who can potentially become the one to take care of your rabbit, remember to discuss your doubts with him/her.

Don't wait for the pet to fall sick. It is always a good idea to choose a veterinarian for the animal in advance. If your pet falls sick or encounters an injury, you should know where to take him. The last thing you want to do is to search for a vet when the pet's condition is deteriorating.

The best way to find a good veterinarian is to go by the breeder's suggestion. A good breeder will always consult a good vet, and will suggest the same to you.

It is important that the veterinarian has good experience of working with bunnies. Many of them might have the knowledge, but might lack in practical experience. It is your duty to make sure that the vet holds a good name amongst other owners of rabbits.

While you are choosing your veterinarian, you should also consider the distance of the clinic and your home. You would want to consult a vet who is good and also close to your home.

3. Common diseases in Netherland dwarf rabbits

This section will help you to understand the various common health problems that your pet rabbit can suffer from. As the caregiver, you should attempt to understand these diseases in detail so that you can provide the animal with the right care.

Pasteurellosis

Netherland dwarf rabbits are prone to Pasteurellosis. It is one of the most common diseases known to affect rabbits across various species. It is also known as sniffles.

It can be controlled easily with the help of a few precautions and measures. Once the pet acquires this disease, it keeps spreading if the condition is not treated.

Cause

The cause of Pasteurellosis or sniffles is a bacterium that is known as Pasteurella multocida. This bacterium attacks the respiratory system of Netherland dwarf rabbits.

It is also known that there are different strains of this bacterium. These strains can have a deadly effect on various parts of the rabbit's body, such as ears and the eyes.

If this disease spreads to the eyes of the Netherland dwarf rabbit, he can acquire Conjunctivitis. On the other hand, if this disease spreads to the ears of the Netherland dwarf rabbit, he can experience head tilting and severe disorientation.

Symptoms

It should be noted that the symptoms of the disease will depend on the strain of bacteria that affect the rabbit. You can look out for the following general symptoms in the rabbit to know if he is suffering from this particular disease:

- The animal will have a runny nose. This is one of the first symptoms of the disease.

- The animal will sneeze a lot.

- If you go near the animal, you will hear him snoring or sniffling while he breathes.

- The rabbit can experience sores or abscesses on his respiratory tract. This will also be very painful.

- He can experience head tilting and severe disorientation.

Treatment

This particular disease can be controlled easily with the help of antibiotics. You should consult a veterinarian as soon as you catch the symptoms of the disease. It should be noted that ignored symptoms can lead to a severe case of Pasteurellosis.

The veterinarian will keep the pet rabbit on a supplementary biotic and antibiotic course for the duration of four to about thirty days. This will depend on the severity of the disease.

Calcivirus

Calcivirus is also known as VHD or viral haemorrhagic disease. Calcivirus is more prevalent in the wild rabbits. It is a viral disease, which can turn extremely lethal if not treated on time.

Cause

The disease is caused by a virus, as the name itself suggests. It can affect the lymph nodes in a very drastic way. In severe cases, the liver can be completely damaged.

If the disease if allowed to spread, it will affect the blood of the animal. The blood will not coagulate. This in turn will affect many other organs of the pet animal.

Symptoms

The following symptoms will help you to confirm whether your pet is suffering from this health condition:

- The virus can lead to inflammation of the intestine, which gets worse with time if it is not treated.

- The pet will also experience high fever.

- As the disease progresses, the pet will lose his energy and will appear more and more lethargic.

Treatment

If you notice any of the given symptoms in your pet rabbit, you should take him to the veterinarian. He/she will take a blood sample of the animal and test it for the disease, along with other tests.

Though the disease can be controlled to some extent, there is no specific treatment for this particular disease. It is suggested to sanitize the habitat of the pet thoroughly, as maintaining hygiene will help to keep this disease-causing virus away from the pet rabbit.

Scours

Scours is one of the most common diseases known to affect rabbits across various species. This condition is characterized by excessive diarrhea in the rabbits.

This is a bacterial disease and can be controlled easily with the help of few precautions. If you give your bunny a proper and healthy diet and also try to maintain optimal hygiene conditions around him, you can definitely avoid this health condition in the pet.

Cause

The main reasons behind scours are unhealthy diet and poor hygiene conditions. If the pet is suffering from a severe case of viral or bacterial infection, scours could be one of the side effects of the infection. In such cases, it is best to treat the infection if you want to treat this condition.

Another common cause of this health condition in bunnies is stress and over-heating. When your pet is going through excessive stress, it will lead to scours.

If there is poor hygiene around the pet, it can also lead to scours. You should try to maintain optimum hygiene levels at all times. If the pet is suffering from some other infection or health condition, scours could be a side effect of the health condition.

Symptoms

The following symptoms will help you to confirm whether your pet is suffering from this health condition:

- One of the early symptoms of this disease includes diarrhea. If your pet is suffering from diarrhea that you are not able to control, then your pet could be suffering from scours.

- You should keep a check on the stools of the rabbit. The color and texture of the stools will help you determine whether the rabbit has scours or not.

Treatment

If your pet rabbit is suffering from excessive diarrhea or scours, you would have to take certain measures to solve this issue. He should be given electrolytes. The electrolytes will help to give the body the salts that it might have lost because of the condition.

It is advised to administer probiotics to the animal. This will help to treat his condition.

Once your pet starts getting better, you should make sure that it is given a very healthy diet. A good diet can prevent scours. You can even consult your veterinarian if your pet doesn't get well. The medication given by the doctor will help the pet to get better soon.

Make sure that all the necessary nutrients are given to the pet. You can also look to give him supplements if his diet does not provide the right nutrition.

Infestation with mites

Netherland dwarf rabbits are also prone to mites. Mites can lead to skin irritation in the beginning and then severe skin allergy if not treated.

It is not a very deadly disease and can be controlled easily with the help of a few precautions and measures. Once the pet acquires this disease, it keeps spreading if the condition is not treated.

Symptoms

You can look out for the following symptoms in the rabbit to know that he is suffering from this particular disease:

- Inflammation of the skin because of the infection caused by mites makes the pet irritable and restless.

- It is a skin disease, so a change in the texture of the skin on the pet could be an indication of an infection. In most cases, the skin starts getting red.

- You will notice dandruff patches on the skin of the rabbit. You should look at the nape of the neck and the base of the animal's tail, where the patches will be very prominent.

- As the condition worsens, the patch size will increase.

- The pet will scratch again and again at one spot. You will find the pet to be very irritated and agitated. The skin could also develop rashes or scales.

Treatment

The skin disease can be treated by the use of mild medicated soaps. These soaps will soothe the skin and will also treat the infection.

There are some creams that can also help to treat the skin and make the condition better. In severe cases, certain ointments might have to be applied to the skin. You should also take care of the diet of the pet.

A good diet will help the skin to heal itself faster. In case the skin gets worse with time then you will have to consult the veterinarian. He might suggest some oral medicines to heal the skin faster.

He might also suggest some special ointments that will give some relief to the pet. The use of 'Ivermectin' is recommended for the rabbits. It helps the skin to get rid of mites faster.

It is also suggested to clean the habitat of the pet after the pet is treated. This is to avoid any relapse of the skin disease.

You should also focus on grooming the animal. This also helps the animal to get rid of dead cells, thus lowering the chance of an infestation of mites.

Urine burn

Urine burn is also common in rabbits. When the urine of the rabbit soaks the fur, it leads to this particular condition.

This can further lead to inflammation of the skin, which gets worse with time if it is not treated. The pet will also experience severe hair loss.

Symptoms

You can look out for the following symptoms in the rabbit to know whether he is suffering from this particular disease:

- Inflammation of the skin because of the infection makes the pet irritable and restless.

- His private areas will appear sore and red. This is one of the most common symptoms of the disease.

Treatment

The burn can be treated by the use of mild medicated soaps. These soaps will soothe the skin and will also treat the infection.

There are some soothing creams and ointments that can help to treat the skin and make the condition better. You should also take care of the diet of the pet.

In case the skin gets worse with time then will have to consult the veterinarian, who may suggest oral medicine.

It is also suggested to keep the habitat of the pet clean. This is to avoid any relapse of the skin disease. The cage needs to be dry and clean at all times.

Pneumonia

The rabbit is also highly susceptible to pneumonia, especially when the bunny is young. If your bunny shows symptoms of a respiratory disorder, you should look for various symptoms of this disease.

It can be caused by bacteria of a virus that thrives in dirty and unsanitary conditions. This is the reason why it is always advised to keep the hutches clean and sanitary.

The main cause of this health condition is damp hutches and cages. If the living conditions of the pet are not good, he can suffer from this disease.

It is important that you treat this disease because it is known to be a life-threating condition. If you discover any respiratory disorders in your pet, you should take the issue seriously because as the disease reaches its advanced stages, it becomes more difficult to treat.

Symptoms

You should be on the lookout for the following symptoms to confirm the presence of the disease in your rabbit:

- If your pet animal refuses to eat, then this could be because of this disease. The pet will suffer a drastic loss of appetite.

- Is your pet being very lazy and lethargic? Is he refusing to move? This could also be because of this disease.

- The pet will have difficulty breathing. There could be a blockage or congestion in the chest area. This is a very common symptom and should be taken very seriously.

- The pet could be suffering from high temperature. This is also a very common symptom accompanying pneumonia.

- The pet might vomit the food that he is fed. This is because of the congestion in his chest.

Treatment

There is treatment available if your rabbit is suffering from pneumonia. The type of treatment that will be chosen will depend on a few factors. If the pneumonia is too severe, then a different treatment is chosen in comparison to if it is not too severe.

The vet will recommend antibiotics to combat the disease. The dose and strength of the antibiotic will depend on the severity of pneumonia in the pet bunny.

If the bunny is not able to recover and is already at an advanced stage, then the dose of antibiotic is injected directly through the skin. This is known to work rapidly on the animal.

Ringworm

Ringworms are a very common issue that can affect your pet rabbit. Ringworms can attach themselves to the rabbit. This will cause immense discomfort to the rabbit.

While many people don't consider this as a major health issue, ringworms should never be ignored. They are known to be very dangerous. They can be a potential threat to your other pets as well. You should make sure that ringworms are treated well and on time.

If you believe that ringworm is a worm, then you are wrong. It is a fungus and fungal treatment is required to get rid of ringworms. If you are treating your pet for worms, then you will not be able to combat this condition.

The problem with this disease is that it can get worse with time, so it is important that you treat it as soon as possible. If ringworms are allowed to grow on the animal, they will lead to a lot of fur loss.

Causes

There are many causes that could be behind the ringworms attacking your pet. One of the most common causes of ringworms is contact with animals already infested with the same.

Ringworms can easily travel from one carrier to another, so if an animal infested with ringworms comes into contact with your bunny, he can easily get them too.

Symptoms

You should be on the lookout for the following symptoms to confirm the presence of ringworms on your rabbit:

- Is your rabbit scratching itself too much? Does your pet seem as if he has an itch? Do you see some area red with itchiness and scratching?

- Do you find him irritable and uneasy? If the answer is yes, then your rabbit could be infected with ringworms.

- Ringworms make the animal itchy and too much itchiness can develop red sores on the body. You should be on the lookout for such obvious symptoms of ringworms.

- The pet will slowly develop bald patches. You should be on the lookout for this symptom. It is one of the most common symptoms of the rabbit being infected with ringworms.

- The head of the bunny is most likely to be affected. It will slowly spread to other parts of the body. You should look out for bald patches on the head.

76

Treatment

If you find the given symptoms on your pet then you can be convinced that your pet has been infested with ringworms. It is important that you take the steps to help your pet get rid of them.

If you do not treat the pet soon, then they will only trouble the poor animal more. You can successfully treat the by following an antifungal treatment for the disease.

You should not allow the pet to come into contact with other pets of the house. The ringworms can spread very easily. Human beings can also easily catch them. You should wear gloves when you go near the pet.

If you find any of the above symptoms in a rabbit, it is important that you waste no time and take the pet to the veterinarian. The vet will conduct some tests to confirm the condition.

He/he will suggest an antifungal cream that will help to get rid of the ringworms. The hair or fur in the affected area needs to be tied so that the ringworms don't spread to other parts of the body.

Hair loss

Another common problem that your Netherland dwarf rabbit can go through is hair loss. Though this might not seem like a big problem, hair loss is generally an indication of other serious problems. Therefore, it is important that you don't take the issue lightly. You should make an attempt to understand the causes of hair loss so that you can work on eliminating those issues.

If your rabbit is very young, hair loss could be an indication that your pet has been kept in extremely warm temperatures. The young pet might not be taking the warn environment well.

If your Netherland dwarf rabbit is not too young, then hair loss could be an effect of some other health issue. You should understand these issues. The most common reasons behind hair loss are unhealthy diet and too much stress.

Causes

One of the most common causes of hair loss in Netherland dwarf rabbits is lack of a healthy diet. You have to make sure that your pet is fed properly so that it can be in its optimum health and glory.

Another common cause of hair loss in Netherland dwarf rabbit is stress. The first things that you should look into after you spot hair loss are the diet and the stress levels of your pet. Apart from these two common causes, there are a few other causes of hair loss in the animal. If your pet is facing some skin allergy or has skin irritation, it can lead to hair loss.

It is also known that fungal infections lead to drastic hair loss. If your pet has suffered from some fungal infection in the recent past, then this could be the cause of hair loss in the pet.

Sometimes, a large amount of bleach is present in soap items. This bleach is harmful for the Netherland dwarf rabbit. You should also check the amount of bleach that is present in the soap that is used to wash things that often come into direct contact with your pet. For example, you can check the amount of bleach present in the soap powder that is used to wash the water container and the food container of your Netherland dwarf rabbit.

Symptoms

The most obvious symptom of hair loss in an animal is the reduction of hair on the body. You might spot hair all over the place.

- If you spot a bald patch on your Netherland dwarf rabbit, then your pet has been suffering from hair loss.

- You should also look for hair loss in bigger and larger areas.

Treatment

If you spot hair loss in your Netherland dwarf rabbit, you should immediately look for the direct or indirect causes behind the same. There can be many causes of hair loss, thus the treatment accordingly varies.

You should make a thorough check on the living conditions of the pet. This will help you to understand the problems that he is facing and the causes behind the hair loss. You might be required to make changes and adjustments on the basis your evaluation. If the cause of the hair loss is food related, then make sure that you work on providing the pet with a wholesome and nutritious diet.

If the cause behind the hair loss is a fungal infection, then you have to make sure that the infection is treated and eliminated. You should apply suitable anti-fungal topical creams for treating the fungal infection well.

If the Netherland dwarf rabbit is stressed, then the most obvious treatment to reduce and stop hair loss will be to reduce the stress of the Netherland dwarf rabbit. You would have to understand the reasons that could be behind the pet being so stressed. You will be required to make appropriate changes in the pet's living conditions to improve his health and reduce his stress levels.

Fleas or lice

As you might know, if an animal is infested with fleas or lice, it can get very difficult and uncomfortable for the animal. Fleas also lead to other issues and problems. Your Netherland dwarf rabbit can catch fleas or lice easily if it comes into contact with other domesticated animals. For example, if you have a pet dog or a pet cat along with the rabbit, then there is a strong chance that your rabbit caught the fleas from them.

Both fleas and lice are parasites that can irritate animals. It can be very easy for your pet to get these parasites, but the good news is that a common treatment can help you to get rid of both these parasites. Another important point that you need to understand is that even after you treat these parasites, the infection can re-occur. It is important to work on the cause of these annoying parasites.

Causes

One of the most common causes of infestation is the contact with animals already infested with the parasites.

Symptoms

The following symptoms will help you to confirm whether your pet is suffering from a parasite infestation:

- The skin of the pet will start to get red. Look for red spots on different areas of the pet. The red areas could also be swollen.

- Does your pet appear itchy? Is he irritated and annoyed? Is he itching more than usual? If the answer to all these questions is yes, then this could be a parasite infestation.

- Does the pet seem visibly irritated? The parasites will make the pet very irritable. He might seem like he is being very moody, but in actual fact it is the irritation caused by the fleas and the lice.

Treatment

If your rabbit is suffering from a parasite infestation by either fleas or lice, you don't need to worry, as it can be treated. You need to make sure that you work on the cause of the parasites also; otherwise the parasites can strike again.

If the other domestic animals in the house have passed on the infestation to the rabbit, then you should make sure that these pets are also treated for the parasite infestation. If you don't do so, there will be a second infestation.

Both fleas and lice can be treated with the same remedy. You would need to apply a special powder to the affected areas of the rabbit. The powder will cool down the area, repair the skin and will also help to disable the fleas and the lice so that they don't create any further damage.

The special powder that needs to be applied on the pet is pyrethrum or carbaryl powder. You can even consult your veterinarian if you think that the infestation is becoming serious.

Coccidiosis

One of the most common health problems in rabbits is the Coccidiosis. This particular health problem is caused by protozoa Cocci, which have only one single cell.

It is important to know that there are nine types of Cocci that can affect rabbits. Eight out of these nine types are known to affect the intestines of the bunnies. The ninth type of Cocci can affect the liver of the rabbit.

You should also know that cats, dogs and chickens can also be affected by Cocci. It is important to note that young rabbits are often more susceptible to Cocci.

Older bunnies have immunity against this disease, so if you have a young rabbit, then you should be worried about this health issue. It is important that you understand the causes and ways to avoid this disease.

Causes

One of the most common causes of this disease is an unclean enclosure. If the cage or the hutch of the rabbit is not cleaned for days, you can expect your rabbit to get infected with this disease.

The parasite will dwell in dirty areas. The rabbit will ingest the egg of the disease-causing parasite. They will do so when they lick or eat from dirty cage floors or when they eat contaminated hay.

While the adult rabbit is less likely to suffer from this condition, it can be a carrier. It can shed the eggs of the parasite in its feces. This can further infect other pet rabbits in the vicinity.

The eggs of this disease-causing parasite can thrive and survive for over a year in a humid and warm environment. This makes it all the more important that you regularly clean the surroundings of the rabbit.

Symptoms

You can look out for the following symptoms in the bunny to know whether he is suffering from this particular disease:

- The pet will lose his appetite. You will find him avoiding even his favorite foods. He will not drink water, which could further lead to dehydration.

- You will notice sudden and drastic weight loss in the pet. This is one of the most common symptoms of this condition.

- Another symptom of this disorder is vomiting. The pet will throw up from time to time.

- The pet would be seen struggling during his bowel movements. You should watch out for this symptom.

- You will notice the bunny being very lazy and lethargic.

- You can spot your rabbit sitting in one corner with a hunched back. His feet will be forward, and he will appear to be really sad and sick.

- The pet will suffer from diarrhea. You might also notice blood in the stools of the rabbit.

Treatment

If you find any of the above symptoms in a rabbit, it is important that you waste no time and take the pet to the veterinarian. The vet will conduct some tests to confirm the condition.

The most common treatment of this condition includes the use of corid powder. You can get it easily at all pet store. Sulfamethoxide is also used to help the pet recover from this condition.

It should be mixed with water and given to the pet rabbit for seven days. After the first cycle, a break of over seven days is taken. After that, the mix needs to be given for another seven days.

Most veterinarians will suggest completing these two cycles at least once in six months. This ensures that the rabbit does not get this health condition again. This is all the more important in young bunnies.

If your female bunny is pregnant, you should not administer this particular drug to the doe. It can be given to her once she is in the lactating phase.

It is important that you don't ignore any symptom and consult the vet as soon as possible. Always try to maintain cleanliness in the hutch of the pet rabbit.

Chapter 7: Training the Netherland dwarf rabbit

It is very important to train the animal to make him more suitable to a household. Give him some time and show some patience.

No matter how much you read about an animal, your pet will have some individual characteristics that will separate him from the rest of the lot. The training phase can be a great opportunity for you to learn more about your pet.

It may take weeks or months before you see any positive results. If you fail to be kind towards him during the training process, he will detest coming to you and things will only get worse.

Don't punish the rabbit if he fails to follow you. You should remember to have fun even during the training phase. You shouldn't be too harsh on your pet.

The pet might slip into sadness and depression if severe training sessions continue. This will hamper the pet's emotional bond with you and also his health.

Rabbits generally associate chasing with being held captive. When you are training the rabbit, try not to chase him.

If you wish to play with them, kneel on the floor. You should be on the same level as the rabbit if you want him to enjoy playing with you.

They will play in your arms for some time and then will want to come down. You should be prepared for such behavior from your pet.

1. Is it possible to train a Netherland dwarf rabbit?

It is imperative to train a pet. It is a way to monitor their behavior and to teach them what behavior is acceptable and what isn't. This is a simple way of helping him adapt to your home and your family.

Apart from teaching him the right behavior, training will also help to form a bond between you and your pet. It will bring the two of you closer to each other.

It is often believed that it is very difficult to train a Netherland dwarf rabbit because he is mischievous and playful. The truth is that it is possible to train the Netherland dwarf rabbit well with continuous efforts.

The sooner you start the training, the better. You should start the training when the rabbit is very young. In fact, you should start the training soon after you bring him home.

You should adopt simple training techniques to train your Netherland dwarf rabbit. If you are consistent, you will get very good results.

If you start the training of the pet from a young age then this will give the pet some time to learn and understand what is expected of him. It is also important that the training is not stopped at any stage. Once you see him picking it up, reduce the intensity but don't stop the training.

When you are training your pet animal, you need to teach him what is acceptable and what is not. It is important to send the right signals to the pet. This is a way of teaching him as to what is expected of him and what is not. The pet will take some time, but will soon understand your instructions.

If your pet tries to bite you continuously then you should give a small toy to the pet. Let him bite the toy. You should repeat this action whenever he tries to bite you. This will send a signal to the pet animal that it is not okay for him to bite you.

When you are looking at training the rabbit, you should be aiming for litter training and training against chewing and biting above everything else.

While you are training your pet, you should remember that the rabbit needs to feel comfortable and secure in your presence. He will only learn when he feels secure with you.

You should spend quality time with him. Don't put him in the cage just to punish him. This will send the wrong message.

If he is left in the cage unattended all the time, he might become very aggressive. This can encourage his chewing and biting behavior. Always remember that they can bite when they are scared and disappointed.

You should never neglect your pet. The rabbit will learn slowly, but you have to be compassionate and kind towards the pet. Treat him when he exhibits good behavior. This will encourage him further.

2. How to train the Netherland dwarf rabbit effectively

If you have a Netherland dwarf rabbit as a pet, you will need to spend a lot of time creating a bond between you. Netherland dwarf rabbits are gentle creatures that make great companions. You can enrich this experience by trying to understand your pet and building a relationship with him.

In this chapter, you will learn how to communicate with your Netherland dwarf rabbit and also the possibilities with having a trained Netherland dwarf rabbit.

Understanding the body language of the bunny

The first step towards building a relationship with your pet is being able to communicate with him. In the case of all pets, verbal communication is the least important tool. What you must focus on mostly is the body language. That will help you figure out the mood and the emotions that your pet is trying to convey, which will make training a lot easier.

Approaching the Netherland dwarf rabbit

Communication can be initiated only when you are able to approach your pet confidently without causing any panic or negative experience for either of you. This section will discuss a few tips to approach a Netherland dwarf rabbit properly and safely.

Make sure that you start slow. Walk towards the Netherland dwarf rabbit slowly and keep the talking to a minimum. The only thing the Netherland dwarf rabbit will focus on is your body and the signals that you are giving out.

Stop at regular intervals and observe the Netherland dwarf rabbit. Does he look comfortable? Does he want to approach you himself? Is he trying to get away from you? If he is moving away, you must stand quietly and let him relax.

After a few moments of no activity, try to approach the Netherland dwarf rabbit again. Make sure that your hands are lowered. Your Netherland dwarf rabbit may want to smell your hand. That is normal. If you hold the hand up, it might seem like a threat to the Netherland dwarf rabbit, who will think that you are going to strike him.

When you get close, your Netherland dwarf rabbit might try to bite you. The scent that you emit is one of the most important things for any pet. This is the first association with a human that the pet will make. So, be as calm as possible and make sure that you do not startle the animal.

Using your body language and words effectively

There are a few things that your rabbit will do that will help you to understand him and his moods better. Some may be signs of inviting you while others are telling you to back away.

For example, if he makes a nipping action with the mouth, this is a sign of warning. The rabbit is telling you that he does not approve of you being too close to him.

It is important that you understand his actions and moods when you are trying to train him. If you force him to learn something, you will only face disappointment. It is always better to give the rabbit some time and space. You will learn more about his actions as and when you spend more time with him.

If the rabbit is running around you and is trying to pull at your leg or pants, this means that the Netherland dwarf rabbit wants something that you have with you. If this habit is not stopped, it can lead to a painful bite in the future. You must stop this with a strong "No". The voice should be clear and loud.

If he rests his head on your foot or stands quietly next to you, this is a sign that the Netherland dwarf rabbit is very comfortable in your presence. This means that the pet is comfortable with you being around, which is a good sign.

If the pet turns his back on you each time you approach him, this is a sign that he is extremely nervous in your presence. When the rabbit does this, do

86

not pet the animal. He might try to hurt you. This can lead to severe injuries if you get too close to the animal.

It is true that rabbits and many other animals do not respond first to verbal communication. The tone of your voice is very important and not so much the words that you use.

Keeping the tone uniform during a certain movement allows your rabbit to read what you and the action means. For instance, if you use the word "no" regularly in a certain tone, he understands that you are not pleased with something.

The pitch of the voice is important. If you keep the voice soft and low, it can have a rather calming effect on the rabbit. You should know that while words are not really a method of communicating with animals, the tone is universal.

However, without any control on your body language and the energy that you are sending out, the tone of your voice cannot help you much when it comes to dealing with these pets. The cues that you give to the animal are of utmost importance.

3. Litter training

As the owner, you are also the caretaker and the parent for the pet. You will have to teach him stuff that he needs to know when living in a family. Don't get upset when you see your rabbit littering all around. You can train him to not do so.

To begin with, you should buy a few litter boxes. Keep these boxes in various areas of the house where the rabbit is most likely to litter. You should cover the various corners where you have found the litter earlier. In addition, install one box in the cage. Eventually, you want the rabbit to litter in the cage itself.

It is believed that a Netherland dwarf rabbit will generally litter in the first fifteen or twenty minutes of waking up. So, there is a chance that the rabbit has already littered in the box in the cage. When you open the cage to take him out, check the box and wait until he has used the box.

You should signal the animal by pointing towards the litter box. The pet should slowly realize that he needs to use the box if he wants to get out of the cage. You should wait near the cage until he is all done.

Another point that you need to understand here is that rabbits are very smart. When the rabbit understands that you will let him out of the cage once he uses the litter box, he might pretend to use it. You need to check the box and make sure that he has actually used it.

If you notice that the pet is not using the litter box installed in his cage, then you need to understand why. There is a chance that the litter box is uncomfortable for him. In such a case, you should look to buy a box with a front ledge that is low. This is good for your rabbit.

You can even make one. If you buy a cat litter box, you will notice that the front ledge is not too low. You could cut it in half to make it suitable for your rabbit. The idea is to make it really comfortable for your pet rabbit. A suitable litter box will have a back ledge that is high. This gives the right support to the pet.

The rabbit will take its own time to adjust to the environment. It is always difficult for a new pet to adjust. If you get him a new cage or if you make any changes in his surroundings, he will find it difficult to adjust, but this problem is only time related and will get solved.

Every time the rabbit litters outside the box, place his litter in the box that he should be using. You need to show the pet that he should be using the litter box. This could be difficult for you in the beginning, but the rabbit will learn soon. You should place food and toys in areas and corners that you want to save.

When the rabbit sees a toy or a food item in a corner, he will try to look for another corner to pass his stool. You can also place a mat underneath the litter box to save your carpet or home mats. Make sure that the mat that you use is waterproof.

Observe your rabbit's mannerisms when he is using the litter box. If he has a tendency to bite the mat underneath or stuff kept around, you should discourage this behavior. To do so, you can use bitter food sprays on the mats and other stuff. This will automatically discourage the pet from biting around when he is littering.

The litter box of the rabbit should definitely be kept clean to maintain the overall hygiene and to prevent diseases. You should wash the box once a week. Yet, a point that needs to be noted here is that the box should not be too clean. A clean litter box that almost appears new could be appealing to you, but it is a turn off to the rabbit.

The rabbit will use its sense of smell to use the areas that he has used before. You should leave some paper litter in the box to encourage the pet to use the box again. This is a simple trick that you can use when you are trying to litter train your pet.

When you are buying a litter box, you should remember that the size of the box will depend on the size of your rabbit. For example, a male pet rabbit will need a bigger box due to his size compared to the box that a female pet rabbit will need.

If you are domesticating more than one rabbit in your home, then this will also affect the littering process of the rabbits. This may come as a surprise to you, but the dominant pet could affect how the other pets use the litter boxes in the house.

You might notice that the habits of a dominant pet rabbit are influencing the other pet rabbits. The dominant one will always try to boss around and make the others feel inferior.

Rabbits don't like to use the same litter box. The rabbits could also be competing for a litter box. These are the issues that you will have to find out. Observe which rabbit is using which litter box and which one suddenly leaves a litter box.

You should make sure that each rabbit has his own box, so that he not left to use the carpets and the floors. Even after you have trained your rabbit to use the litter box, you have to be vigilant.

If you are observant, you might face issues. There could be instances when your pet would suddenly give up the use of the litter box. Instead of getting angry at him, it is important that you probe into the reason for his sudden change in behavior.

When the pet is sick, he might give up the use of the litter box. The main reason behind this is that the pet might not have the strength in his hind legs to get on to the box. He could be suffering from a gastro intestinal or adrenal disease, which could make him weak and lethargic.

You should be cautious when you observe such changes in your pet rabbit. Don't ignore his condition, or don't force him to use the litter box. You should not get angry with the pet because he is littering on the floor. It is not his fault if he is not well.

The best thing to do in such a situation is to take the pet to the vet. This will prevent the condition getting worse. He/she will look for the symptoms of various diseases and will help you to understand what is wrong with the pet.

The given process will take some days, but you will have to have some patience. The idea is to help the pet get used to the food before you can expect the pet to eat the food. Once he is gets used to it, he will try out the food item on his own.

4. Nip training

When you buy a Netherland dwarf rabbit, you might notice that the animal has a tendency to bite. This can be uncomfortable and worrisome for you as the owner, but you should know that this is absolutely normal for a Netherland dwarf rabbit and that you can slowly train the rabbit not to exhibit such behavior.

When you know what you can expect from a new pet, it gets easier. Try to understand that he is still uncomfortable in the new surroundings and will require some time to get used to all that is new around him. Give him that space, time and also your understanding.

The first thing that you should remember is that you should not harm the pet when he bites. This could scare him and will make things worse for you. If you mishandle the pet and try to beat him, he might also try to bite you and harm. Avoid going down this road and aim at training the Netherland dwarf rabbit well.

It is important that you understand the reason behind a pet's biting. More often than not, Netherland dwarf rabbits do so when they are in a playful mood. If the pet wants you to play with him, he could just signal you to do so by biting.

Another reason behind a pet's biting is that the animal could be scared. When you bring the pet to your home for the first time, everything around him will be new. It is quite natural for the pet to get scared. This is the reason that biting is very common in a new pet Netherland dwarf rabbit.

As explained earlier, a rabbit can exhibit such behavior when they are scared. There are many rabbits that are beaten up and abused. If you have rescued one such animal, then you will definitely find him trying to bite you out of fear and tension.

However, don't worry because this is a passing phase. The love and warmth he will get at your place will help him to come out of his history of beatings and abuse.

If the pet is very young, he needs to be taught the behavior that is expected of him. He needs to learn to be sociable. He needs to learn that it is not okay to bite people. There are some tips and tricks that will help you to teach him all this.

Every time the pet tries to bite you, you should loudly say the word 'no'. Do it each time, until the pet starts relating the word 'no' to something that he can't do. Don't beat him because this will only scare him. Just be stern with your words and also actions.

If think that the above trick is not very useful, then you can put the pet in his cage for some time. The pet will eventually understand that this behavior will send him into the cage. The word 'no' and the act of putting into the cage will make the pet more cautious of his behavior.

As mentioned earlier, you can also give him a toy to bite on every time he bites. This teaches him what is acceptable to bite and what is not.

It should be noted that it will take some time for the pet to understand this. Until then just be patient and keep repeating these actions each time he tries to nip you. The pet will call back on his memory eventually and relate the cage with something punishable.

Chapter 8: Grooming and showing the Netherland dwarf rabbit

It is important to groom a Netherland dwarf rabbit in order to ensure that the coat stays smooth and shiny and the pet stays in the best of health. If you plan to enter your pet bunny into shows, grooming is particularly important. You will have to dedicate time for grooming sessions in order to keep the pet clean and healthy.

1. Grooming the Netherland dwarf rabbit

You should understand that when you pay attention to the basic cleaning and grooming of the pet rabbit, not only will your pet appear neat and clean; he will also be saved from many unwanted diseases.

When you are looking at grooming sessions for your rabbit, you should pay special attention to the pet's ears, nails, coat, teeth and bathing. This chapter will help you to understand the various dos and don'ts while grooming your pet Netherland dwarf rabbit.

It should be noted here that the Netherland dwarf rabbit will not require frequent bathing, but regular brushing of the coat is important to keep the wool in good condition. If you fail to groom the pet regularly, you will put the wool and the skin of the pet at risk.

If you are domesticating the rabbit for its wool or for showing the rabbit, then it is very important that you groom the pet nicely. Grooming the pet rabbit is also necessary to maintain the hygiene and well being of the pet. Even if the pet will not participate in shows, you should make sure that he is neat and clean at all times.

Most rabbits are easy to handle. This nature of the pet makes it very simple for the caregiver to groom the pet. However, you should understand that much will depend on the individual personality of your pet.

You should start the grooming sessions with the pet when he is very young. When you start a grooming session with the adult rabbit, he might take some time to get used to the new routine.

On the other hand, if you start when the pet is very young, you give him some time to get accustomed to frequent grooming sessions. This is good for you and the pet in the long run.

You should take special care of the Netherland dwarf rabbit's wool. The wool needs to be combed regularly to maintain the health and luster of the same. If you don't comb it regularly, you will see the wool getting tangled.

Once the wool is tangled, it can be a real pain for you to get rid of these tangles. You will have to apply pressure and force, which can be very uncomfortable and painful for the pet rabbit.

It is important to note that this can cause the bunny to shed loose tendril of its wool. This is a warning signal for you as the caregiver of the pet that something is not right with the health of the rabbit.

Netherland dwarf rabbits have the tendency to groom themselves. They will lick themselves like cats. This can cause the bunny to swallow some of the hair or wool. The rabbit is unable to cough this ball of hair like cats do.

This can lead to a serious health issue called wool block. The hairball remains inside the pet's body in this condition. This can lead to many complications if the condition is not treated on time.

The rabbit feels that his stomach is full because of the presence of a hairball in his stomach. This makes him lose his appetite and he eats less. This can be really detrimental for the overall health of the pet rabbit.

It should be noted that this condition is rare in Netherland dwarf rabbits, but still you need to be prepared.

You should help your pet in this condition by feeding large quantities of hay because it has fiber. You should also make sure that the pet rabbit drinks a lot of water to help him during this condition.

Cleaning the ears

It should be noted that while certain rabbits are prone to various kinds of ear infections, many others aren't. The rabbits with erect ears are less prone to such infections. On the other hand, smaller ears that are not open are more prone to ear infections.

An erect ear type gets enough airflow to save it from infections. Netherland dwarf rabbits have erect ears. Their ears are open and allow good airflow. While the design of the ears help the Netherland dwarf rabbit to ward off infections, you also need to do your bit.

It should be noted that wet ears are susceptible to bacteria. The bacteria can grow in the ear and lead to various diseases.

The ears of the Netherland dwarf rabbit also need to be cleaned regularly so that there is no wax deposited in the ears. There are many owners who might not consider ear cleaning an important part of pet keeping, but in reality wax can lead to mite infestation and other infections.

In severe cases, the hearing power of the pet can be compromised. It is important that you know of the early signs of mite infestation. The wax in the ears will have a light brown color, while the wax with mites will be dark brown in color.

It is important to see the veterinarian in case you have doubts about mite infestations. Don't put any drops in the pet's ears without consulting the vet. In general, you should try to clean the pet's ears once a week, or at least once in ten days.

You will require a cotton swab and an ear cleaning solution that is used for rabbits. If there is somebody in the house who could help you, it will be easier to clean the ears.

If you are the only one doing this task, you should be calm and patient because Netherland dwarf rabbits don't like their ears being touched and cleaned. You can warm the cleaning solution before use.

Sit comfortably on the floor and hold the Netherland dwarf rabbit gently by the loose skin behind the neck. Use your lap to give support to the pet's legs. Take a cotton swab and apply some cleaning agent to it.

You should use the cotton swab with the cleaning agent to clean the parts of the ear that are easily visible to you. Don't go too deep because this can hurt the pet. You should definitely not try to go further in the ear canal.

Repeat the process on both the ears. If you commit a small mistake from your side, it could cost the Netherland dwarf rabbit his hearing. So, you need to make sure that whatever you do is gentle, yet with firm hands.

The Netherland dwarf rabbit might get uneasy and might try to get away from your grip. To make sure that the pet is stable and not jerking, you can give him a treat. This will keep him occupied and will make your job easier.

Trimming the nails

It is important to cut the nails of the Netherland dwarf rabbit regularly. You should be looking at doing so at least once a month. If the nails of the Netherland dwarf rabbit are not cut on a regular basis, there is a chance that the nails will get stuck somewhere. This will cause the nails to get uprooted.

You can imagine the pain your Netherland dwarf rabbit will have to go through if the nails are uprooted. You will have to rush to the veterinarian to help the Netherland dwarf rabbit. Not only this, but the long nails can also leave marks and scratches on your skin. So, make it a point to cut the nails of the pet regularly.

You should also make sure that you use the right equipment to cut the nails of the pet Netherland dwarf rabbit. You should use good quality animal nail clippers. Along with that, you would need a soap and styptic powder.

You can give some treats to the pet rabbit. This is to distract the animal so that he does not disturb you when you are busy clipping his nails.

If there is someone else in the house, you can ask them to hold the Netherland dwarf rabbit. If you're on your own, place the Netherland dwarf rabbit in your lap in a way that he is comfortable and you have access to his nails.

You will notice a reddish vein on the nail. This is called the quick. You should cut the nail in a way that the quick is not touched. If you happen to hurt it, it will hurt the pet and will also bleed.

In case you cut the nail in way that the quick starts bleeding, use soap to clean it and then apply the powder. This will give relief to the pet. You should give a few minutes to the Netherland dwarf rabbit to feel better before starting the process of clipping the nails once again.

Cleaning the teeth

Taking care of the teeth is an important part of grooming the Netherland dwarf rabbit. As the owner of the Netherland dwarf rabbit, it is important for you to know that the teeth of the rabbit are always growing. If you pay attention you will realize that the teeth sometimes become so big that the rabbit has difficulties in eating.

When you are considering the overall hygiene and cleanliness of the Netherland dwarf rabbit, you also have to take care of his teeth. You might have problems cleaning the pet Netherland dwarf rabbit's teeth in the beginning, but he will get used it quickly.

As a rule, you should try to clean the Netherland dwarf rabbit's teeth once or twice a month. If you ignore his teeth, you will only invite unwanted problems for the Netherland dwarf rabbit. You will notice tar depositing on the teeth if they are not clean. This will automatically lead to tooth decay.

Many owners complain that the pet closes its mouth while the teeth are being cleaned. This makes it very difficult for the cleaning to take place. If your pet does this, then you can clean only one side of the mouth in one sitting. This means that you will have to be more frequent with the teeth cleaning sessions.

It is also important that you take the pet to the vet if you see any tar on the teeth. Even if all seems fine, it is advised to schedule dental check-ups for the Netherland dwarf rabbit once or twice a year. The vet will trim the teeth of the pet if there is a need.

To keep the teeth clean on a regular basis, you can find toothpaste specially designed for rabbits. Along with the toothpaste, you should use a soft brush that has been specially designed for them. A toothbrush with hard bristles might hurt the pet's jaw, so you should avoid using it.

Your movements should be very soft. If you are too hard, you will hurt the Netherland dwarf rabbit. Be very observant of the lather that comes out from the pet's mouth. If you see a pink or red color, you should immediately know that it is blood and that you are being too hard on the bunny's mouth.

Brushing the coat

It should be noted that brushing the coat of the Netherland dwarf rabbit is essential. You should make sure that you brush the coat of the animal regularly. This will help to ease out the tangles in the hairs of the rabbit.

Regular brushing of the coat will also help you to get rid of dust from the coat. This is important to keep the Netherland dwarf rabbit neat and clean. You need a brush with soft bristles. Hard bristles can harm the pet, so avoid such a brush. You can buy a good brush online at a cheap price or from a local pet shop near your area.

Netherland dwarf rabbits have short coats. You need to brush the coat regularly to avoid any fur balls. If you are regular in brushing your rabbit's coat, you automatically eliminate the need to bathe him on a regular basis.

Bathing the Netherland dwarf rabbit

Netherland dwarf rabbits belong to the class of animals that are not extremely fond of bathing. However, the good news is that these animals do not require regular bathing. There are a few species of rabbits that need to be bathed every now and then, but your Netherland dwarf rabbit does not.

Though the pet does not require regular baths, it is important that you understand the circumstances under which the pet should be bathed. You should also lay emphasis on how the bath should be given. It is important that the pet is handled with care and love. Don't be forceful and have some patience with the poor animal.

Bathing is known to be a very stressful event for Netherland dwarf rabbits. They don't take it well. They also take a lot of time to dry. The wet coat can actually lead to diseases such as pneumonia.

However, this does not mean that the pet should be left dirty. If the pet is not clean, he will attract fleas and other parasites. This only means extra work for you and veterinarian visits for the rabbit. Make sure that the pet is well groomed to avoid such hassles.

The frequency of a bath should depend on the climate and the environment of the bunny. If it is too hot or if the surroundings are not too clean, it means that your pet should be given a bath more often than a bunny that resides in cleaner and cooler environments.

Sometimes, a veterinarian will advise you to bathe the Netherland dwarf rabbit. This could be to cool his body and to lower his fever, if he is sick. Schedule a bath once every few weeks. The rest of the time you can use wet wipes to clean the rabbit of any dirt or dust.

Bathing is also important to keep the coat of the rabbit clean. This is important to maintain good quality wool of the pet. If you don't clean the coat, the rabbit gets prone to many skin diseases.

If the rabbit is shedding its wool tendrils, the excess wool might stick on to the body. When you give the pet a bath, the loose tendrils will just get washed off with water. This also means that the fur will not be shed all over the house.

When you are looking to give a nice bath to your rabbit, you should be looking at two things: a good quality and mild shampoo and a few towels. It is very important that you choose the right shampoo for the Netherland dwarf rabbit.

If the shampoo is too hard or harsh, it will leave rashes on the rabbit and might even cause serious damage to his skin. This makes it important that you invest in buying a mild shampoo.

You can easily get a good quality shampoo online or in the pet store. Make sure that the shampoo that you choose is very mild on the skin and has proven to be ideal for the Netherland dwarf rabbit.

You can take a small amount of shampoo and test it on a small part of the skin of the rabbit. This is to make sure that the shampoo is safe for the pet. If you see the skin reacting, then you should make sure that you avoid this shampoo.

You also need a few towels handy for the Netherland dwarf rabbit. They will help to dry the wool of the pet nicely.

There are a few precautions that you need to take. You should understand that how your rabbit behaves in water will depend on its individual personality. It is important that you make a few attempts to understand your pet's personality. Don't give up and understand his behavior and mannerisms. This will only help you in your future dealings with the pet.

You should always remember that while it is fine to bathe the rabbit once in a while, over-bathing is not recommended. This can also create many problems. The skin of the pet will begin to lose many important essential oils if they are bathed frequently.

If your Netherland dwarf rabbit is suffering from flea infestation, then you will have to use a shampoo that can help the Netherland dwarf rabbit get rid of the fleas. You should consult the veterinarian before you use a specialized flea shampoo. It is important not to take a chance on the health of the pet.

It is important that you make a few attempts to understand your pet's personality. Don't give up and understand his behavior and mannerisms. This will only help you in your future dealings with the pet.

To begin with, make sure that the water you are using to bathe the pet is warm. Netherland dwarf rabbits can get stressed very easily. They will detest cold water. They should be bathed in warm water to keep them safe.

Take a tub and fill it half with warm water. Lift your Netherland dwarf rabbit delicately in your hands. Make sure that your grip is firm. The pet might surprise you when it touches water and might try to jump out of your hands. To avoid such a situation, place your hands on the stomach area and hold him firmly.

Place the Netherland dwarf rabbit in the tub of warm water for a few seconds. Observe how he responds to water. If you see him enjoying, then your work becomes easier. You can also sprinkle water over the pet. But, if the pet is not enjoying then you need to be quick.

Take him out of the water, and put some shampoo on his back. You should form a good lather with your hands from the ears towards the tail region. Make sure that the pet does not escape when you are shampooing it. You need to have a firm grip on him.

You can also make use of the kitchen sink to give the rabbit a bath. The sink will be deep and it will be difficult for the bunny to run away. The pet is hydrophobic, so it is advised to use to two sinks or tubs. Fill both with water and use them alternately. Keep talking to your pet and make him feel that everything is fine.

Another way to bathe your hydrophobic Netherland dwarf rabbit is to sway him under running warm water. Turn the tap on and make sure the water is warm. It should not be cold or too hot. Once you are convinced that the temperature of the water is right for the pet, hold the pet and bring him under the water for a few seconds.

Before he starts to get fidgety, take him away from the water. Now apply some shampoo over the Netherland dwarf rabbit. Keeping swaying him under the water until all the shampoo is washed off. It is very important that all the shampoo is washed off; else the pet's skin will get affected and will show signs of rashes and abrasions.

After the bath is done, place the bunny in a big towel. You should place a few blankets or towels on the floor to keep it warm and tight for the animal. The Netherland dwarf rabbit will show too much energy at this time. He will try to escape you. You should be very gentle with the pet, otherwise you could harm him.

While you are bathing the Netherland dwarf rabbit, it is important that you protect his face. Water should not enter his eyes or ears. These are sensitive areas and water could cause some damage to them. Keep him on the towels and use another towel to pat him dry. Make sure that he is absolutely dry before you let him go, otherwise he will stick dust and dirt on his skin.

Giving a full bath to the Netherland dwarf rabbit is not an easy job. While it is difficult, it is also not very good for the pet. The pet can get dry skin, which can further lead to many skin related problems and other diseases.

More often than not, the pet owner is forced to give a bath to the Netherland dwarf rabbit because he has soiled his feet or coat. If you don't clean the feet, the Netherland dwarf rabbit can soil other areas and can also get an infection.

If you are trying to get rid of this problem, then you can give a footbath instead of a full bath. For a simple footbath, fill a water tub or sink with over half an inch of water. Make the pet walk in the tub or sink. This will help him to get rid of the poopy boots.

You can also wet a big towel or a paper towel and make the Netherland dwarf rabbit walk on it. You can also use baby wipes if you want to get rid of dirt or a little amount of grime. This is a simple way to avoid a full bath. You can also use these baby wipes to clean off the dirt from this skin and coat.

2. Showing the Netherland dwarf rabbits

Netherland dwarf rabbits are adorable pets, but they are capable of being more than just household pets. There are many owners that keep and domesticate Netherland dwarf rabbits to make them take part in shows. These shows are extensively popular amongst many rabbit lovers.

If you also wish to keep or domesticate the Netherland dwarf rabbit for the purpose of showing, then you need to make sure that you follow certain guidelines. There are certain breed standards that your Netherland dwarf rabbit needs to qualify for.

The American rabbit breeders association (ARBA) has set some guidelines that will help you to prepare your Netherland dwarf rabbits to participate in such shows. You should make sure that you understand these guidelines. These guidelines will help you not just in preparing your rabbit for the show, but also to take good care of the pet.

Rabbit shows give you the opportunity to showcase your rabbit and also win a potential prize. These shows will also help you to meet other rabbit owners. You can connect and exchange notes about your pet animals. This is a great opportunity to broaden your horizons and know more about your breed of rabbit and also other breeds.

It should be noted that you can't suddenly wake up from a slumber and decide to participate in shows. Even if you do so, you will not gain much from the shows. If you are serious about showing your rabbit, then you will have to prepare all year round.

You need to take proper care of the rabbit. You will have to make sure that everything about the bunny is on point. There are many people who take rabbit shows very seriously. They prepare religiously for them. So, it is advised that you prepare well or just quit participating in such rabbit shows.

This chapter will help you understand some breed standards for the Netherland dwarf rabbits. You will understand how to keep and present the pet in the best possible way. Certain tips for the shows will also be shared. You will learn what needs to be done before the show and on the day of the show.

Breed standards for the Netherland dwarf rabbits

The BRC has set total 100 points for judging Netherland dwarf rabbits. Out of these 100 points, 30 points are for body, 15 points for ears, 15 points for head, 5 points for eyes, 15 points for color, 10 points for coat and 10 points are for the condition of the rabbit.

The BRC also has the right to disqualify your rabbit from the rabbit show. The rabbit can be disqualified if it is not healthy or is overdeveloped for its age. It can also be disqualified if it has crooked legs, runny eyes, mutilated teeth, odd color, putty nose, white patches and white armpits.

Preparing for the show

You need to be a member of an organization. The ARBA organization and BRC organization are the two organizations that will allow you to be a member and also enter a show with your Netherland dwarf rabbit. You can register with either of the two organizations.

The process to become a member is fairly simple and straightforward. You need to approach the organization and show an interest in being their member. You should also register your pet under your Netherland dwarf rabbit name.

Once you are a member of the organization, you will be intimated with all the latest happenings and shows in your area. You should be alert regarding the requirements and deadlines. The registration process can take some time, so don't wait until the last minute to get it done.

If you want to enter a show with your Netherland dwarf rabbit, you will have to make sure that your rabbit is in its best form. You should take care of the health and well being of the animal and make sure that he is ready for the contest.

After you are sure that your rabbit is ready to take part in the contest, you can plan on getting him admitted for the show. Always keep checks on the shows happening in your area. You should check if your rabbit fits the requirements.

When you find a show that allows your breed of rabbit to take part in the contest, you should go ahead and register your rabbit. Register your rabbit in the show that you find relevant and suitable.

Though most rules are quite standard, it is always advised to be careful so that your rabbit is not disqualified from the show or subsequent shows. You should also note the deadlines related to the application and other things. It is always better to be prepared before the main show day.

Once you have registered for the show, you need to make sure that you and the pet are ready. Make all the necessary arrangements to get to the venue much before the final day.

After the rabbit is registered to participate in the rabbit show, the wait for the final day begins. You have to ensure that you have all the necessary documents and a copy of the exact schedule with you. You should know the exact time when your bunny would be showed. Having these things handy will help you to avoid the last minute rush and tension.

Final show day

There is nothing much that you need to do from your side on the day of the show. It is advised to take the opportunity and observe other bunnies. This will help you to understand Netherland dwarf rabbits in a better light. This will go on to help you to take better care of your pet rabbit.

While you have done your part for the preparation for the show, there are a few pointers that will help on the final day of the rabbit show. This section will help you to understand the procedure of judging the rabbits on the day of the show. It is important not to panic and to understand things well. It is just a show. You need to learn from it and also enjoy it.

When you apply for the show, you will be told by the organizers whether your rabbit qualifies for the show or not. You need not worry, as you will get plenty of time to prepare for the main event. While you are taking good care of the pet Netherland dwarf rabbit and preparing well for the rabbit show, you should also prepare a handy kit. This kit will help you on the day of the show. Your kit should have all the items that the bunny or you might need on the final day of the show.

You should securely keep the registration form of the pet in the kit. You will need to show it at the venue. You should keep your business card with the form. Make sure that you keep a towel, some paper wipes, nail clippers and a slicker brush. You can also keep scrap carpet squares and hydrogen peroxide for emergency grooming and cleaning of the bunny.

It is also a good idea to keep a collapsible stool. This will be essential when you know that chairs won't be available. You should also keep some fresh food and water for the bunny on the day of the show. Apart from packing the essentials for the rabbit, don't forget to carry food and water for you. You need to take care of yourself so that you can take care of the rabbit.

After your rabbit has been confirmed for the main show, you will be told about the start time of the show and the time of judging the rabbits. You will also be assigned a pen by the organizers. You are supposed to keep the rabbit ready to be judged in the assigned pen. It is always better to reach the venue earlier. Once you reach the venue, look for the assigned pen for your bunny.

If you wish to understand the procedure of these rabbit shows then you should know that the process of the judging in a rabbit show is quite simple. It is same across all competitions. The judges will visit all the pens one by one. They will judge the bunnies on various parameters, such as coat health, eyes and ears.

You are not expected to do much when the rabbit is in the competition ready to be judged. You should relax and enjoy the show. You should just make sure that the rabbit is in the pen at the time of judging. The last thing that you want is your rabbit sneaking out at the time of judgment. A bunny that is not in the pen will obviously not be judged.

After all the rabbits are evaluated, the judges will exchange notes and announce the winners of the show. The winners would be chosen keeping in mind all the parameters set for the competition.

If your rabbit wins a prize, a card will be left by the judges on the pen your pet rabbit is in. Once the entire process is over, you can take the card and get the equivalent prize money from the reception area.

Once you get your prize money, you are free to leave the rabbit show. If you wish to, you can also spend more time and connect with other owners. You can share notes with these owners. Irrespective of the result of the show, you should make sure that you make the most of this opportunity. You can discuss your issues and doubts regarding the pet with other owners.

It is always a good idea to learn from the experience of other people. These rabbit shows allow you to do so. You can also help other owners learn from your own experience. This is a great way to form a close-knit community of rabbit owners that can help each other.

Conclusion

Thank you again for purchasing this book!

I hope this book was able to help you in understanding the various ways to domesticate and care for Netherland dwarf rabbits.

Netherland dwarf rabbits are adorable and lovable animals. These animals have been domesticated for many years. Even though they are loved as pets, they are not very common, and there are still many doubts regarding their domestications methods and techniques. There are many things that prospective owners don't understand about the animal. They find themselves getting confused as to what should be done and what should be avoided.

A Netherland dwarf rabbit is a small, naughty animal that will keep you busy and entertained by all its unique antics and mischiefs. It is said that each animal is different. Each one will have some traits that are unique to him. It is important to understand the traits that differentiate the Netherland dwarf rabbit from other animals. You also have to be sure that you can provide for the animal. So, it is important to be acquainted with the dos and don'ts of keeping the Netherland dwarf rabbit.

If you wish to raise a Netherland dwarf rabbit as a pet, there are many things that you need to understand before you can domesticate the animal. You need to make sure that you are ready in terms of right preparation. There are certain unique characteristics of the animal that make him adorable, but these traits can also be very confusing for many people. You can't domesticate the animal with all the confusions in your head.

If you are still contemplating whether you want to domesticate the Netherland dwarf rabbit or not, then it becomes all the more important for you to understand everything regarding the pet very well. You can only make a wise decision when you are acquainted with all these and more. When you are planning to domesticate a Netherland dwarf rabbit as a pet, you should lay special emphasis on learning about its behavior, habitat requirements, dietary requirements and common health issues.

When you decide to domesticate an animal, it is important that you understand the animal and its species well. It is important to learn the basic nature and mannerisms of the animal. This book will help you to equip yourself with this knowledge. You will be able to appreciate a Netherland dwarf rabbit for what it is. You will also know what to expect from the animal. This will help you to decide whether the Netherland dwarf rabbit is the right choice for you or not. If you already have a Netherland dwarf rabbit, then this book will help you to strengthen your bond with your pet.

The ways and strategies discussed in the book are meant to help you get acquainted with everything that you need to know about Netherland dwarf rabbits. You will be able to understand the unique antics of the animal. This will help you to decide whether the Netherland dwarf rabbit is suitable to be your pet. The book teaches you simple ways that will help you to understand your pet.

Thank you and good luck!

References

Note: at the time of printing, all the websites below were working. As the internet changes rapidly, some sites might no longer be live when you read this book. That is, of course, out of our control.

http://www.nationalgeographic.com

www.ehow.co.uk

http://www.mnn.com

https://en.wikipedia.org

http://www.runningbugfarm.com

http://joyofhandspinning.com

http://small-pets.lovetoknow.com

http://www.rabbit.org

http://www.mnn.com

http://www.handallhousefarm.com

http://twotalentshomestead.blogspot.in

https://hub.co-opinsurance.co.uk

https://www.popsugar.com

http://ipfactly.com

https://www.petcha.com

http://www.petrabbitinfo.com

https://www.peta2.com

http://www.raising-rabbits.com

http://www.petguide.com

https://joybileefarm.com

http://www.wikihow.com

https://www.thespruce.com

https://www.pets4homes.co.uk

http://www.hobbyfarms.com

www.bbc.co.uk

https://www.cuteness.com

www.training.ntwc.org

http://animaldiversity.org

https://a-z-animals.com

https://www.theguardian.com

http://www.businessinsider.com

Made in United States
Troutdale, OR
11/21/2024

25127018R00066